NARROW GAUGE AT WAR

by Keith Taylorson

Plateway Press, 13 Church Road, Croydon, Surrey, CR0 1SG

ISBN 0 9511108 1 0

British Library Cataloguing in Publication Data

Taylorson, Keith
    Narrow Gauge At War
    1. Military railroads – Great Britain – History
    2. Military railroads – Europe – History
    3. Railroads, Narrow gauge – Great Britain – History
    4. Railroads, Narrow gauge – Europe – History

    I. Title
    385'.52'094   UG345

    ISBN 0-9511108-1-0

Printed in Great Britain by Wayzgoose Ltd., Boston Road, Sleaford, Lincs.

Front cover: "Steam Gives Way to Petrol." Baldwin 4-6-0T No. 778 and 'protected' Simplex No. LR3102, at an interchange point in France, 1918. Detail from a watercolour by Roy Link, inspired by a photograph by W.W. Dunning: 'artistic licence' has been employed to transform the identity of the locomotives into two examples now preserved at Chalk Pits Museum, Amberley, West Sussex.

Frontispiece: Baldwin 4-6-0T No. 647 hauls a trainload of men and supplies, somewhere in France, c. 1917.   *(A. Neale collection).*

Preface

The last few years have seen an upsurge in interest in military light railways, and a renewed appreciation of the role which narrow gauge railways played in servicing the battlefields of World War 1 – the 'War to end all wars' which reached its bloodiest peak of intensity just 70 years ago. Interest has shown itself in the creation of military railways in model form and also in the preservation of surviving 'prototype' equipment: two War Department Light Railways Baldwin 4-6-0T's have recently been 'repatriated' to Britain, after over 60 years of exile on Indian sugar plantations, and there are plans to return one (LION Blw 44656 of 1916) – to workable condition at the Chalk Pits Museum, Amberley, West Sussex in the near future.

A number of books have dealt with the W.D. Light Railways in varying degrees of detail (see Bibliography, page 55). The standard work is W J K Davies' "Light Railways of the First World War", and it is unfortunate that this most scholarly and readable work is no longer in print. This book in no way attempts to replace "Light Railways of the First World War", nor does it purport to be a definitive history. Rather, it seeks to present, in words and pictures, a portrait of the War Department Light Railways as they developed to meet the needs of a war effort that had strained existing modes of transport to breaking point.

In choosing the illustrations, I have concentrated on those which show the light railways at work, and have used these to describe how the 60cm gauge railways developed to form an integrated, professionally-run transport system, with ultimate uses far more varied than envisaged in their original remit. I have attempted to select illustrations not previously published, the exceptions being photographs of particular technical merit or historical interest. Because of the wealth of superb material available, this volume deals exclusively with operations on the Western Front (France and Belgium). This, of course, represents only a part of the story, and it is intended that a future volume will portray military light railways on the 'home front', and W D L R and Allied Army activities in other theatres of War.

* * * * * * *

Any writer tackling the subject of War Department Light Railways owes a debt of gratitude to earlier generations of researchers: published sources consulted by the author are listed in the Bibliography. The quotations from Arthur L Stead's reminiscences were reproduced from THE LOCOMOTIVE magazine, originally published by the Locomotive Publishing Co., with kind permission of their successors, Ian Allan Ltd. Thanks are due to the staff of the Department of Photographs, Imperial War Museum, for their help in locating photographic material.

In compiling the captions to the illustrations I have been greatly helped by the specialist knowledge of Mike Chappell (military history) and Andrew Neale (locomotives) and the latter was responsible for the various Appendices at the end of the book. Responsibility for any errors of interpretation or fact is, of course, entirely mine.

The cover artwork and the map are the work of Roy Link, and photographic work is by Tim Shuttleworth of Brookside Photographic Services, Shrewbury.

Acknowledgement for assistance of various kinds is due to:- A M Burgess, K W Clingan, G W Green, B J Hawkesworth, R T Horne, G Horsman, I B Jolly, F Jux, P N Lowe, R N Redman, D H Smith, M Swift, J L Townsend, Lens of Sutton, the Narrow Gauge Railway Society, the Industrial Railway Society, the Industrial Locomotive Society.

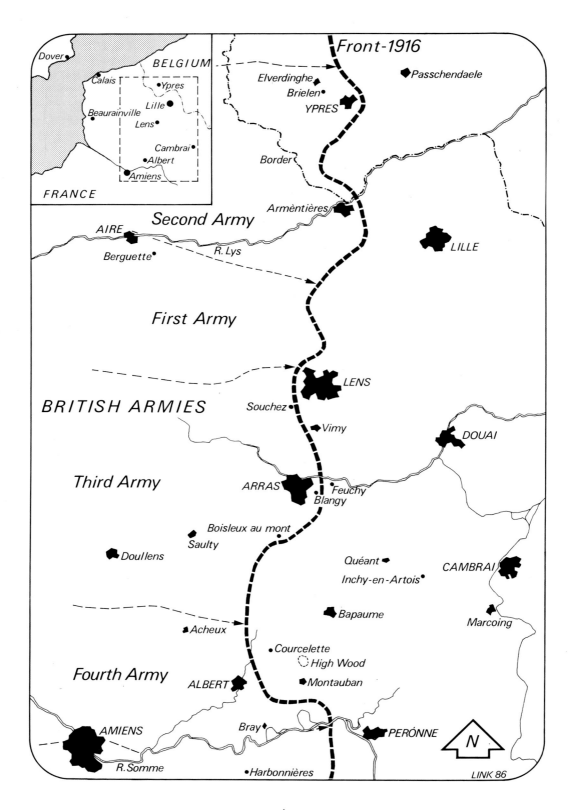

Dover•

BELGIUM

Calais•
                •Ypres
        Lille•
Beaurainville•
        Lens•

            Cambrai•
        •Albert
    •Amiens

FRANCE

Front-1916

Elverdinghe•   •Passchendaele
    Brielen•
        YPRES

        Border•

            Armèntières•

Second Army

AIRE   LILLE
    •
Berguette•   R. Lys

First Army

BRITISH ARMIES

                LENS
        Souchez•
            •Vimy
                        DOUAI

Third Army

        ARRAS•   •Feuchy
                Blangy

        Boisleux au mont•
        Saulty
    •Doullens   Quéant•
                        •Inchy-en-Artois   CAMBRAI

                    •Bapaume
            •Acheux   Marcoing
                    •Courcelette
                    ◌ High Wood
Fourth Army
    ALBERT•   •Montauban

AMIENS   •PERÓNNE
            Bray•
    R.Somme   N
            •Harbonnières   LINK 86

Introduction

The role of tactical light railways as an 'engine of war' spanned a period of 70 years, from the 1850's to the end of World War 1. Military railways were a by-product of the Industrial Age, which made mechanised war possible and – it can be argued – inevitable. That same process accelerated the development of the motor vehicle, resulting in virtual extinction of the tactical light railway after 1919.

The first military railways were the result of local 'improvisation.' During the Crimean War, men of the Royal Corps of Sappers and Miners[1] used civilian contractors to build a primitive 7½ mile line from Balaclava to Sebastopol, which proved capable of transporting 700 tons of material a day. In 1867, R.E. and Indian Army Engineers were sent to Abyssinia where 10th Co. R.E. laid 12 miles of track from Zula on the Red Sea towards the interior, rising 350 ft. from sea level and including construction of eight girder bridges. During the Sudan campaign (1896–98), Royal Engineers working from a base at Wadi Halfa in Egypt, constructed 370 miles of railway across hostile country in 15 months, contributing significantly to the eventual British victory.

At home, the War Office was applying its official mind to the tactical use of the light railway. In 1874, trials were held at South Camp, Aldershot, of a system developed by J.B. Fell, involving prefabricated track on trestles, designed for rapid erection and adaptation on the battlefield. This, and experiments using a device known as a 'Handyside' which could act as locomotive or stationary engine, were failures. The Royal Engineers continued to follow narrow gauge developments in this country, including Sir Arthur Heywood's 15″ gauge line at Duffield Bank – Heywood's 'Minimum Gauge' was conceived with military requirements in mind – but the War Office, unimpressed, made no provision for tactical railways in future conflicts.

Other major Continental powers were also considering the military uses of light railways. Impetus was given by mass-production of 'portable' railways by the Decauville company. Although the railways were designed for agricultural use, their

1. *A typical German Army light railway operation: a 'Feldbahn' 0–8–0T heads a train of bogie opens containing troop reinforcements.*   *(R.N. Redman collection)*

potential in wartime was recognised by the War Ministries of France, Germany and Russia, who all laid in stocks of Decauville equipment (some saw use during the Russo-Japanese War). Similar equipment was produced by the German firm of Arthur Koppel.

While the French had a primarily 'defensive' philosophy, and used narrow gauge railways principally to supply their frontier forts, and to transport artillery to extend their fire power, it was the Germans who saw the real value of light railways in war, that of maintaining the flow of supplies to the front line during an advance. Until standard gauge railways could be repaired or extended, a railway that could be quickly laid down would be needed. Experience of operating 60 cm gauge railways was gained in South-west Africa in 1897–1907, and the Germans began to stockpile locomotives, wagons and stock in preparation for the next European war.

The British Army, meanwhile, used 18″ gauge railways within military establishments such as Woolwich Arsenal, and on construction projects, but maintained no stocks of 'war' equipment. This was due not to conservatism but to a premature assessment of the efficiency of motor lorries. 1913 Army Regulations officially sanctioned lorries as the approved method of moving stores from railheads to forward units. Also, the prevailing military philosophy centred around a 'war of movement' spearheaded by cavalry – in 1914 combined Allied armies fielded some 50 cavalry Divisions. In the words of the Official History "......in anticipation that the War would once again become one of movement.....it was considered wasteful to embark on an extensive system of light railways which might soon be left far in the rear". But the nature of war itself was about to undergo a profound change.

By the end of September 1914 the initial German advance had been checked at the Battle of the Marne, and in October the first battle of Ypres presaged the stalemate that was to endure for 3½ years. Both sides dug in, and the entirely new phenomenon of trench warfare was born. Throughout 1915 and 1916, the opposing armies decimated themselves in fruitless frontal attacks. The awesome power of the machine gun made cavalry obsolete, and turned assaults by infantry into organised slaughter. Frustrated, the Generals turned to technology. Poison gas, grenades and mines were added to arsenals. Artillery reached new heights of destructiveness, with bombardments of ever-increasing intensity: for the attack at Verdun in 1916, the Germans brought up 2,500,000 shells, using 13 trains. By June, the artillery of both sides at Verdun had grown to 2,000 guns, and in four months of combat 24,000,000 shells had been pumped into this one battle area. For the Somme offensive of 1916, the British 4th and 5th Armies deployed 2,029 guns on a 14-mile front. In an eight day bombardment, they fired off 1,732,873 rounds. After 153 days of bombardment and battle, the British guns had fired 27,768,076 rounds, equivalent to 3,951 tons of ammunition per day[2].

2. This picture, issued as a 'Daily Mail' postcard, graphically illustrates the conditions which paralysed road transport in the front-line areas.

(Author's collection)

Huge tonnages of food and water for armies of millions of men had to be transported. Trench warfare also created its own specialised demands: picks and spades to dig trenches; timber to shore them up; barbed wire; pumps and pipes, duck boards and sandbags, telephone cables, rockets, lights . . . the list was endless, the demands ever more strident. Up to 1916, movement of supplies to the front lines was carried out by the armies themselves, using lorries, horses, and fatigue parties. Carrying capacity of the latter was low, and diverted manpower from the front line. Horse transport was also labour-intensive and was vulnerable to artillery and gas attacks. Consequently, more motor lorries were pressed into service, but this caused increasingly serious problems.

The primitive lorries of 1914–18 with their narrow, solid tyres were effective road-destroying machines. The consequent potholes, unless mended quickly, would deepen and soon make the roads impassable. French roads were founded on chalk, and as the pounding of thousands of wheels added to the natural hazards of frost and rainfall, the foundation would break up, a chalky ooze appear on the surface, and the road quickly disintegrate into a morass. By 1916, maintaining the roads had become beyond the capabilities of the French, and British Army personnel had to be diverted onto this task. Furthermore, so much petrol was being diverted to France for Army use that shortages developed at home. In August 1916 Lloyd George (Secretary of State for War) warned the C-in-C, France that "unless we can effect some economy in petrol, we shall be faced with a curtailment of motor bus services, which . . . would interfere with getting work-people to and from the large munitions factories."

The initial solution was to push standard gauge railheads closer to the front line, so that horse transport could cope with distribution. However the growing range of artillery made this impossible. *Henniker* neatly sums up the dilemma:–

> "a standard gauge railway overtaxed with traffic cannot sort out individual trucks from a train load of ammunition and deliver them at a number of different railheads; all that can be done is to send complete trainloads to one railhead. At the time of arrival at the railhead, the demand might be for a nature of ammunition of which the train brought little or none. There must therefore be a dump at the railhead as a reservoir into which ammunition not required at the time of its arrival can go and from which deficiencies can be made up. The railhead must be fairly safe from shell fire; consequently it must be some way back from the front and will almost always be beyond the reach of horsed transport[3]."

The solution – so obvious once adopted – was the 60 cm gauge railway.

3. The first deliveries of narrow gauge equipment to the front line took place when the light railways were still operated by the Railway Operating Division (R.O.D.) of the Royal Engineers. Hunslet 4–6–0T No. 309 still bears its R.O.D. designation in this February 1917 view at Elverdinghe, near Ypres, a town which was one of the nodal points of the 1914-18 conflict. After savage battles in April–May 1915, in which poison gas was used to deadly effect by the attacking Germans, Allied forces remained in control of the town and a three mile salient to the east, which was used as a springboard for the 1917 offensive. In the intervening two years, the front was largely static, becoming an ideal proving ground for the newly formed Light Railway Operating Companies as they perfected the techniques of building and operating light railways.

The train in this official photograph (Q1695) conveys a working party of troops engaged in trench and fortification maintenance, an unceasing task in an area subject to regular artillery bombardment. They are being conveyed in 'D' class wagons, designed to carry 10 tons of goods but often used to carry personnel on maintenance work. No. 309 was one of the original delivery of what was to become the most popular of any of the steam locomotives used on the British light railways. Developed from the 'Hans Sauer' class, an 0–6–0T built for the Ayrshire Gold Mine and Lomagunda Railway Co. Ltd. of Rhodesia in 1905, the additional front bogie allowed room for a bunker behind the cab and spread the axle loading. Capable of hauling 286 tons on the level or 80 tons up a 1 in 50 incline, they were a typical British Edwardian narrow gauge locomotive, the only concessions to wartime austerity being the lack of a running plate around the boiler and smokebox.

The success of these soon caused the inital order for 45 locos to be increased to 75, and undoubtedly more would have followed had Hunslet had the capacity to meet this sudden huge demand. However as they took 13 months to deliver these locomotives, the subsequent very large orders for steam locos were placed in the U.S.A., a total of 495 to the same outline specification being built by Baldwin, and another 100 similar 2–6–2T's by Alco. (Imperial War Museum)

VICTORIOUS BUT TIRED.

Canadian Official

4. *Another contemporary postcard ('Daily Mirror' series) shows Canadian wounded being transported on a typical trench 'tramway'.*

(Author's collection)

From the beginning of the 'static war' in 1915, difficulty in moving shells and supplies had stimulated development of 'trench tramways', using wooden rails of 3'' by 2'' section laid on sleepers of 1'' planking, produced in sawmills set up by R.E. Field Companies. Wheelsets for the home-made trucks were obtained from the coal-mining area around Bethune or the factories of Armentieres, where primitive tramways of this type were in use. Owing to their quiet running on noiseless rails, these railways could be taken right up to the front line. Following takeover of sectors from the French army, systems using 9lb/ yd and 16lb/yd track also began to develop, these were legitimised in a Circular issued by the Quartermaster General in September 1915. Another Instruction (February 1916) sanctioned construction of 60cm gauge lines "where their necessity could be clearly demonstrated." The QMG's order of 4 August 1916 stipulated that light railways should be used on the whole front for carriage of traffic in the following order of priority (a) heavy gun ammunition (b) lighter ammunition (c) engineer stores and (d) supplies.

By mid-1916 the whole transportation system – from ports and harbours, through the overburdened French railway system, to the final distribution network – was in imminent danger of collapse. The whole war effort was threatened. Sir Eric Geddes, a Departmental Director at the Ministry of Munitions, and formerly Deputy General Manager of the N.E.R., was called in to report on the Transportation organisation. Among his fundamental reforms he recommended that tactical light railways be developed to serve the forward areas. Geddes can rightly take credit for forcing the War Office to appreciate the viability of light railways, though in essence he was doing no more than accelerating the pace of existing construction, and ensuring that more resources were committed to light railway development.

The War Office made wide-ranging changes in organisation, leaving the Railway Operating Division (R.O.D.) responsible for running the standard gauge railways, and putting the running of light railways under a Director-General. Thirty Light Railway Operating Companies (L.R.O.C.'s) were formed – twenty in England, six from existing units in France, and four Dominion Companies (two South African, one Canadian and one Australian). A training course was improvised at Long-moor, although recruits with a 'railway' background were sought where possible to simplify the training commitment.

5. *A works train headed by 'armoured' Simplex No. 2192 plus three 'protected' Motor Rails in a quiet sector of the front.* *(Lens of Sutton)*

8

6. The crew of 4–6–0T No. 359 (Hunslet 1271) pose proudly with their locomotive at a base camp some-where in Belgium. No. 359 is coupled to a train of 'E' and 'D' class bogie opens while in the distance a pair of 'Hudsons' and an Alco simmer away at the servicing point. Judging by the Hunslet's immaculate condition, the photograph was probably taken soon after its delivery in mid-summer 1917. No. 359 was part of the third batch of these locomotives ordered by the War Office on 6th October 1916 under order no. 37930 and delivered between 24th March and 22nd October the following year. As events turned out, these were the last group of Hunslets to actually see military service in France, the next forty being intended for use on the Italian and Middle Eastern fronts, while the end of hostilities meant that none of the final order for 40 more locos placed on 11th July 1918 were actually delivered before the end of the War four months later.

Hunslet 1271 is fitted with a section of rolled steel joist as a re-railing bar both front and back, but later members of this batch and all subsequent locos of this type had this feature replaced by a length of flat bottom rail. The final locomotive in this order (Hunslet 1287, WDLR 375) was fitted with condensing gear and a steam pump with feed well behind the rear foot step. This was an attempt to cut down smoke and noise so that these locos could work further forward than hitherto. Although its trials at the Longmoor Military Railway were quite successful, by the time they were completed, petrol locomotives had proved their worth for forward area duties and the idea was dropped, No. 375's condensing equipment later being removed.

Both 359 and 375 were among a number of these locos bought by Honeywill Bros. after the War. Ross and Constantine Honeywill were the sales agents for the Kent Construction and Engineering Co. Ltd. of Ashford, who specialised in the rebuilding and resale of ex WDLR equipment, particularly Motor Rail locos. No. 359 was subsequently resold to a South American railway, whilst No. 375 was one of five of these locos despatched to Hunslet in 1925 for rebuilding to 3′0″ gauge and subsequent use by Balfour Beatty on their Lochaber Aluminium Works contract in Fort William, western Scotland.   (Imperial War Museum)

Massive orders were placed for locomotives, track and rolling stock: the initial programme called for 1,000 miles of 20lb/yd track, 700 steam and 100 petrol tractors, and 2,800 wagons.

By March 1917, networks of new 60 cm gauge lines were developing on most of the British fronts. Mileage of new lines constructed during 1917 and 1918 was as follows:-

	1917	1918
Jan–March	135	214
Apr–June	364	202
July–Sept	328	297
Oct–Dec	195	73
	1,022	786

7. *Barclay 0–6–0WT No. 619 shunts three 'H' class water transporters, two of which are camouflage-painted.*   *(R.T. Horne collection)*

The light railways played a valuable part in the battle of Passchendaele in 1917: following an attack on September 28th resulting in an advance of 6–8 miles, track laying commenced the same day towards Passchendaele and Gheluvelt. Both lines were linked up to existing German systems and by October 1st L.R.O.C. trains were carrying ammunition into Passchendaele village. By November, operations were even slicker: during the Cambrai offensive, a 60 cm line built by No 2 Army Tramway Co. R.E. was working into Marcoing the day after its capture.

First-hand accounts of operations on the W.D.L.R. are scarce, but in 1946 Arthur Stead, an officer with the Light Railway Directorate in France, wrote an account of his Wartime experiences. Stead begins:-

8. *20HP Simplex No. LR2393 trundles a wagon along a lightly laid track in the front line area, 1918.*   *(Lens of Sutton)*

"Coming from a highly efficient standard-gauge railway undertaking, one certainly found working on the narrow-gauge railways in France curious in the extreme, but as time went on most of us learned to love our quaint 'Heath Robinson' systems, with their crazy track and their diminutive locomotives and wagons, and the utility of the 60 cm gauge network under the peculiar conditions prevailing rapidly became apparent. Day in and day our, often working right round the clock, the 60-centimetre locomotives handled their huge loads of troops and supplies, their utter reliability and ability to take punishment without complaining providing a remarkable testimonial to builders and operators alike."

9. Once it became obvious that English builders could not produce steam locomotives in the quantities required, the War Office sought suppliers in America. By chance the Baldwin Locomotive Company were just building eleven 4-6-0 side tanks for the 60cm gauge French military light railways in Morocco and as these generally met the War Office specification for 4-6-0T's, 45 were immediately ordered in August 1916, although simplified in some details such as a half instead of a full cab. As Baldwin's price (£1,475 free on board, New York) and delivery were so favourable, when the big light railway expansion began in the autumn, a further 350 were ordered, and then yet another 100, the whole lot being delivered by April 1917, a truly impressive achievement when it is remembered that production of other locomotives was in full swing at the same time.

The 10-12-D class was of typical American design with bar frames, outside cylinders and Walschaerts valve gear, stove pipe chimney, a steam dome with two pop safety valves and a large boiler mounted sand box. There were no running plates and the side tanks rested on 'trays' braced to the boiler/firebox assembly and coupled by yokes over the boiler top. As the locos were intended for a short, hard existence, their makers were amazed when the War Office insisted on copper, not steel, fireboxes and brass tubes. While they were a highly successful design, hindsight showed that a 2-6-2 wheel arrangement would have been better, as there were few opportunities to turn the locomotives when in service, so cab first running with its attendant rough riding had to be tolerated.

This picture (Q35517) taken somewhere in Belgium in 1917 shows No. 799 (Baldwin 44704 of 1917) posing with a train of D class bogie wagons at a forward area yard. Another Baldwin has just arrived with a similar train in the background, while an 'open' 40HP Simplex and a Hudswell 0-6-0WT are waiting to take over. On the right is a row of Dick Kerr and Westinghouse petrol electric locos.

(Imperial War Museum)

"The busy period was from dusk to dawn, and locomotive crews seemed to develop a sort of sixth sense which somehow or other carried them through. Train crews consisted of a driver, fireman and guard. There being no brake vans, the guard rode in between the last wagon and the last wagon but one, from which precarious position he manipulated the hand brakes as required. Much of the 60-centimetre rail system was single-track, with telephone-controlled passing loops. Derailments were a nightly event, and working on a derailment in pitch blackness under the very nose of the Germans was no sinecure.

10. *"One certainly found working on the narrow gauge railways in France curious in the extreme . . ." An L.R.O.C. soldier prepares to hand-start 'protected' Simplex No. 2217.* *(Lens of Sutton)*

Drivers and firemen in time became expert at rerailing locomotives, but in each Army area there were special breakdown trains for use in emergency."

To illustrate the life of a typical L.R.O.C., Stead recalls his experience with one such unit having its headquarters at Maroeuil, near Arras:–

"The personnel were accommodated in sandbagged huts in the standard-gauge goods yard, and the company's locomotive shed and wagon shop were similarly protected. The distant traffic control was located a mile or two to the east, at Artillery Corner. Front-line positions at the time were placed about five miles east of Maroeuil, and the job of the light railways was to convey troops and supplies from standard-gauge railhead to the infantry and artillery before Arras and on the Vimy Ridge.

"Altogether the company operated about twenty miles of track, with about sixteen outside control posts. These posts, usually staffed by two men each, were located in dug-outs, and at times these also served as dressing-stations for walking wounded from the trenches. We handled about 1,000 tons of traffic with our steam and petrol locomotives every 24 hours, and looking back it seems miraculous how sometimes we managed to keep traffic moving with enemy shells falling all around, sometimes half-burying train crews in the debris. Many of the routes were under direct enemy observation and could be worked only at night."

11. *"Drivers and firemen in time became expert at rerailing locomotives . . ." Alco 1290 in trouble, somewhere in France, 1918.* *(Lens of Sutton)*

12. This Australian official photo (E. (Aus) 1216) depicts a squad of the Australian Pioneer battalion returning to their dugouts during the Ypres campaign in 1917. Each Division had a Pioneer battalion who were used for a variety of simple (labour-intensive) field engineering tasks such as road-making, trench digging, wiring etc. but they could also be used as infantry when necessary. Torrential rainfall was an unfortunate feature of this campaign and the surrounding quagmire is typical of front line conditions – the consequent value of efficient railway communications will be easily appreciated.

The locomotive is Alco 2-6-2T No. 1273 (works number 57163 of 1917) one of a batch of 100 supplied by the American Locomotive Corporation between February and March 1917. Although a heavy locomotive (17 tons) they were able to run on the lightly laid 20lb/yd rails as can be seen in this picture. Although the cabs were more substantial than on their Baldwin 4-6-0T counterparts, they did not give full weather protection, and the crew of No. 1273 have rigged up a tarpaulin to keep out the constant rain (this would also mask glare from the firebox at night). Note the water-lifter hose on the running plate (left), used to obtain water from rivers, streams or shell-holes when no 'official' water supplies were readily available.

Known to their crews as "Cookes" after the plant at which Alco built them, they were the most powerful locomotives in service on the light railways. The 2-6-2 wheel arrangement meant they ran equally well in either direction, an important advantage over their Hunslet or Baldwin counterparts. Superficially similar to the Baldwins, particularly the US Army 2-6-2T's, they are distinguishable by the lower set boiler, lack of stay rods from smokebox to front running plate and generally more angular appearance. A number saw post War service on French sugar beet lines, including the Festiniog Railway's MOUNTAINEER which was originally WDLR 1265 (Alco 57156 of 1917).   (Imperial War Museum)

13. *A captured German Army Deutz 4wP is placed aboard an 'F' class wagon for shipment to a repair workshop.*

(Lens of Sutton)

Later, Stead describes operations on a portion of front between Bethune and Armentieres, on a system which expanded as they took over tracks abandoned by the retreating Germans:–

"Working over the Nieppe Forest line in the night was a terrifying experience. The single track followed the course of the battered main highway through the forest, with branches here and there leading to artillery batteries concealed in the trees. At the northern edge of the forest, the light railway emerged at a point bearing the significant name of 'La Rue des Morts'! (Street of the Dead)."[4]

By 1918 the light railways were operating at maximum efficiency, with a peak of 205,000 tons conveyed over 834 miles of track in February. There was a decline following the German offensive in April, when some lines were overrun and locomotives destroyed or captured, but by August, traffic had built up again to 140,000 tons on 747 miles of track.[5] After the Armistice, the Army wound up the L.R.O.C.'s as quickly as it had created them, and although some n.g. lines, under Army control, continued to operate on reconstruction work up to the mid-1920's, the tactical use of light railways ended, in Europe at any rate, in 1919. During the 1930's the French built lengthy underground networks of overhead electric lines to serve the Maginot line, but these were never used 'in anger' as the frontier fortifications were neatly bypassed by the German *Blitzkrieg*, apotheosis of the 'war of movement' that had failed to materialise 25 years earlier.

14. *Motor Rail Simplex No. 2184, one of the first 'armoured' locos built. Conditions inside the shut-down loco are scarcely imaginable.*

(Lens of Sutton)

REFERENCES

1 Incorporated in the Corps of Royal Engineers in 1856.

2 "White Heat: The New Warfare 1914–1918" John Terraine

3 "Transportation on the Western Front" HMSO

4 "The Locomotive" September 14 1946

5 "Light Railways of the First World War" W J K Davies

15. For all the combatants the supply of water for steam locomotives was a constant problem. It was usually impractical to provide permanent fixtures such as water towers, as they would be an inviting target for enemy artillery or air attack. The problem was usually tackled by fitting the 'main line' locos (Hunslets, Baldwins and Alcos) with a water lifter and a long length of hose through which water could be drawn from any convenient ditch or shell-hole. Inevitably the Germans were rather better organised. All of their 2,500 odd 'Feldbahn' 0-8-0T's were fitted with similar water lifters and pumps but in addition they built around 300 bogie tenders which could be used with whichever locomotives were currently being employed on longer hauls.

In this Official view (Q35470) at an unknown location in France in 1918, a Baldwin 4-6-0T is seen drawing water from an 'H' class bogie tank wagon. These wagons consisted of a standard bogie underframe on which was mounted a rectangular enclosed rivetted steel tank capable of holding 1,500 gallons. Water could be pumped out via a manhole cover at each end of the top, but unlike their French equivalents the British wagons had no hand pump. A further point of interest in this picture is that the 4-6-0T illustrated (Baldwin 45194 of 1917) is one of the last 145 built which had their cast iron number plates carrying WDLR nos. 1005 to 1150 replaced by a new number series 546 to 700 painted on to a simple wooden plate. The picture appears to have been taken at a loco servicing area as at least five more Baldwins can be seen in the left hand background. (Imperial War Museum)

Locomotive Development

The British and Dominion forces ultimately employed around 1500 locomotives on the War Department Light Railways, more or less equally divided between steam and petrol engined locomotives. Considering that British narrow gauge lines of the period, public and industrial, were probably less standardised than anywhere in the world (and were to remain so) it is remarkable that this total was only divided into 10 basic types, five each of steam and petrol. Nevertheless this still compares badly with the Germans whose far larger fleet had only the three basic steam loco types – including no less than 2500 of the famous 'Feldbahn' 0-8-0T's, built by 19 different firms but all exactly alike – plus a range of Deutz petrol locos.

Some 2'6'' gauge material had been built for the War Department at the beginning of the War; this was intended to service a 'siege' type operation, and with the advent of the static trench war, some orders for this equipment were cancelled. However, some were used in the Middle East campaign, worked by Avonside and Hawthorn Leslie petrol locomotives, much of it having been intended for the ill-fated Gallipoli campaign. Once the need for light railways in France was established there was a brief argument as to which gauge to employ, orthodox army theory considering 2'6'' to be the ideal gauge, with 1'6'' as an alternative, but the existence of a considerable French Army network, some of which was being taken over by the British, soon established the need to use the 'standard' Decauville gauge of 60cm (1ft 11⅝in). This debate over, the initial orders for railway equipment in March 1916 seemed likely to be delayed, as British manufacturing capacity was taken up with orders for the French artillery railways, but at the end of that month the War Office decreed that their orders would take priority.

16. *A pleasing portrait of No. 425, one of the later 'Hudson' 0-6-0WT's, probably taken in 1918.*
(Lens of Sutton)

For the first locomotives, Rendell, Palmer and Tritton, the War Office's consulting engineers, went to Robert Hudson Ltd of Leeds, who with their German rivals Orenstein & Koppel were the largest manufacturers of light railway plant in the world. Unlike Koppel, Hudson only built rolling stock and trackwork, subcontracting locomotive orders to builders such as Hunslet and Hudswell Clarke. Fortunately Hudson had a suitable design for a shunting locomotive readily available in the form of the 'G' class Hudswell Clarke 0-6-0WT (see Plate 17). The tender for 'main line' steam locomotives was won by the Hunslet Engine Co. who offered a suitable modification of their 'Hans Sauer' 0-6-0T. To meet War Office needs a leading bogie was added spreading the axle load and allowing a bunker to be fitted. 45 locomotives were immediately ordered, followed by 30 more later in 1916 (Plate 3 and 6). Both Hunslet and Hudswell produced good workmanlike locomotives which were well up to the job. However British loco builders were accustomed to producing 'one off' locomotives or small batches at the most, and with pressure of other war work and a depleted staff they had no hope of meeting this sudden, unprecedented demand. Although subject to much criticism from the chairbound 'experts' at the War Office, in all fairness Hunslet did remarkably well to design and build the initial order for 45 locos in 13 months.

Nevertheless the huge demand had to be met somehow. For well tanks Andrew Barclay Ltd. at Kilmarnock were able to offer a modification of their standard 'F' class 0-6-0WT, and 25 of these were therefore ordered and delivered early in 1917 (Plate 19). For more 4-6-0T's it was necessary to look overseas, as every British builder was booked for months ahead with essential war work. The Ministry of Munitions therefore turned to the Baldwin Locomotive Company of America for a further 45 locos. By chance, Baldwin were then building 60cm gauge 4-6-0T's (class 10-12-D) for the French military railways in Morocco, and as this met the War Office specification, were able to offer delivery by December 1916.

17. This picture (CO2106) shows the Canadian Army Yard at Dixie siding, near Vimy, following the capture of Vimy Ridge – so long an impregnable barrier to the Allied forces – by Byng's Canadian Corps on April 9th 1917. Running light through the yard is an unidentified 'Hudson' 0-6-0WT. Although marketed by Robert Hudson Ltd of Gildersome, near Leeds, and carrying their name on the works plate, these were actually built by Hudswell Clarke and Co. of the Railway Foundry, Leeds. The design goes back to 1911 when Hudson asked Hudswell to design a range of standard types of four and six coupled well tank of varying size. Closely resembling designs by Hudson's great German rival Orenstein & Koppel they were intended to counter the severe competition from that Company, with a cheap simple locomotive ideal for contracting, mine and plantation work, the well tank between the frames giving a very low centre of gravity and hence stability on poorly laid track.

The War Office locos had 6½in × 12in outside cylinders and a tractive effort of 2909lbs, being rated by Hudsons at 30HP. Starting with an initial batch of six in June 1916, a total of 77 were ultimately built for military use, including 25 for the Salonika campaign and 11 for projects in Britain. Like all their builder's products, they were competently designed and well built proving popular with the troops who used them. The inital batch of four (WD Nos. 101 to 104, Hudswell Clarke 1112–1116) arrived in time for service on one of the earliest British light railways in the Fricourt area during the first Somme offensive by the 3rd and 4th Armies in July 1916. After the War a number were bought back by Hudsons for rebuilding and resale and are recalled as arriving back at Hudswell's in a terrible state, platework badly battered and well peppered with shrapnel holes. Despite this, many put in another 40 to 50 years service on industrial railways in countries such as France, Palestine, Mauritius and India. (Imperial War Museum)

The design was simplified to facilitate mass production notably in the design of the side tanks and substituting a half for a full cab (plates 9 and 15). When the big light railway expansion began in Autumn 1916, Baldwin were asked to build another 350 locomotives, and with their enormous manufacturing capacity, were not only able to deliver the whole lot by April 1917, but when asked by the MoM, built another 100 within this timescale as well. However not even Baldwins could keep pace with the demand, particularly as at the same time they were meeting all their normal home and export orders, and large orders from the other Allies for steam and petrol locos. Hence another American firm, Alco, agreed to build 100 more steam locos. This time, the opportunity was taken to build them with the 2-6-2 wheel arrangement, as experience with both makes of 4-6-0T had shown them to be rough riders when running bunker first (Plate 12).

18. *Light Railway Operating Compay troops pose with their British Westinghouse 4wPE No. LR2036.* *(Lens of Sutton)*

For something more flexible and versatile in use, capable of being readied for service at once, and not prone to give their position away to the enemy by emitting steam, smoke and sparks, petrol locomotives were the answer. Unlike the motor car, production of commercially practical petrol locomotives was an untried art in 1914. Only one firm, Baguley Cars Ltd., and their subsidiary McEwan Pratt Ltd. had any real experience, and the fact that a suitable design was ready and waiting was due to the foresight of one man, Mr. T. Dixon-Abbott, Managing Director of the Motor Rail & Tramcar Co. Ltd. Founded in 1911 with a works at Lewes, Sussex, Motor Rail built petrol-electric tramcars and small inspection vehicles. On holiday in Germany before the War, Abbott had noted the large German stock piles of military light railway equipment. Convinced that a war was imminent he designed a small petrol locomotive, suitable for mass production, a virtually unknown concept in England at that time except for the Ford Model T car. The essence of his locomotive was his patent gearbox which allowed the same number of speeds in each direction, as opposed to the several forward speeds and one low reverse speed of conventional motor vehicle transmission.

Tragically no one in the War Office was interested, despite Abbott's persistent lobbying. However, once the need was recognised, Motor Rail were able to immediately begin production of their 20HP Simplex 'tractor'. A simple, rugged machine powered by a Dorman 2JO petrol engine on a cableless, channel steel four-wheeled underframe, a total of 950 were produced between August 1916 and the end of hostilities (Plate 21). For longer hauls something more powerful was needed so Motor Rail designed a larger version having the 40HP Dorman 4JO engine. This had a similar transmission but a much wider frame of plate steel. For use in the battle zone, 'protected' and 'armoured' versions were built (Plate 23). Motor Rail's Lewes works was too small to produce locos at the rate the Army demanded them so space was rented at the works of crane manufacturers the Bedford Engineering Co. as well as subcontracting out manufacture of many components. Ultimately in 1918 the Company opened their own premises in Elstow Road, Bedford which they still occupy today. At the peak of wartime production output was running at 20–25 locos per week.

Initial War Office plans were for steam locomotives to undertake the 'main line' work and overhead wire electrics to operate in the exposed forward areas where steam locomotives' noise and smoke would attract enemy fire. One Hunslet 4-6-0T was experimentally fitted with condensing gear (page 9), however the success of the big Motor Rails made this and the plans for overhead electrification unnecessary, and the 200 electric locos were actually built as self-contained petrol electrics.

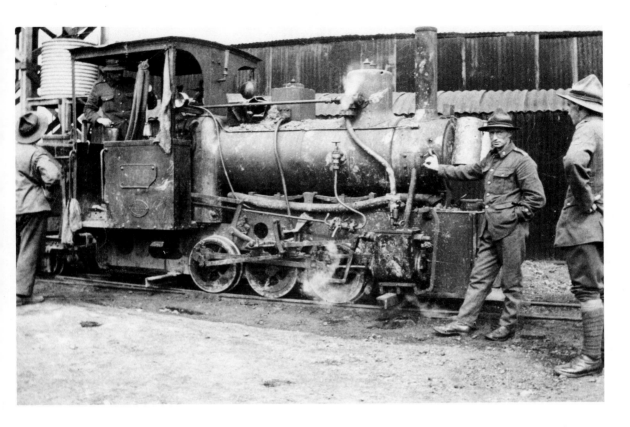

19. Despite building an additional erecting shop especially for the WD well tanks, Hudswell Clarke were unable to meet the Army's demands for the 'Hudsons' and so in August 1916 the Ministry of Munitions ordered a further 25 0-6-0WT's to the same general specification from Andrew Barclay and Co. Ltd. of Kilmarnock. No doubt Barclay were chosen as they already had a suitable design available in the form of their 'F' class 0-6-0WT. However as neither of the two standard variants (7in × 11in and 8½ × 12in cylinders) quite met the Ministry's requirements, a modified design was built with 6¾in × 10¾in cylinders, 4ft 2in wheelbase and 1ft 11in diameter wheels. For cheapness and utility only a plain stovepipe chimney and the minimal cab were provided but in all main respects the original design was retained.

Being relatively few in number, they were rarely photographed and far less is known about their history than any of the other WDLR locos. Apparently they were used exclusively by the Australian Light Railway Operating Company, who found them so serviceable that they carefully transported them when assuming responsibility for another area of the front. A number of New Zealand troops went to Gallipoli as part of the ANZAC Corps but after arrival in France operated as an independent NZ Division. In this undated picture, New Zealand Army Engineers pose with a battlescarred example of the class. Note the rerailing bars, designed to prevent the locomotive falling between the tracks in the event of a derailment, and the locally improvised side sheets fitted to the rather exposed cab.

Although in the post War period Barclay sold a number of their 'E' and 'F' class 0-4-0 and 0-6-0 well tanks, no more of the WD version were built. However a maker's photograph of WDLR 602 (AB 1519) appeared in contemporary Barclay sales literature, carefully 'doctored' so that a more elegant chimney appeared to be carried rather than the ugly stovepipe that was there in reality!   (R.T. Horne collection)

Two firms built these machines: Dick Kerr & Co. of Preston, and British Westinghouse, each producing 100. The latter firm subcontracted the mechanical parts to Nasmyth Wilson & Co. Ltd. who in turn passed the work on to the Leeds Forge Co. Ltd. Although generally similar, the two types had detail differences, notably in the design of the frames. The trusty Dorman 4JO engine again provided the power through a generator to two nose-suspended axle hung traction motors, a pioneering design familiar today in the British Rail 08 class diesel shunter built by Dick Kerr's successors, the English Electric Co. Ltd. The original overhead wire concept was not totally forgotten for the locomotives were designed so that the petrol engine and generator could be shut down and power taken from an outside source. To this end, trolley pole sockets were fitted although never actually used. Designed to run in pairs, cab to cab (but capable of operating singly) they were also used as mobile generating sets, as was originally intended. Well built and reasonably successful, their main fault was their slowness, a major disadvantage in a locomotive exposed to work in front line areas.

20. *A rarely seen view of surplus WDLR equipment stored at Purfleet in 1919: several Baldwin 4-6-0T's and one Hunslet 0-6-0WT are visible.*

(F. Jones collection)

The remaining two types of petrol locomotive were attempts to provide motive power for the trench tramways with their light 9lb/yd rail but neither could be regarded as a success. Baguley Cars Ltd. produced a four coupled locomotive using their own 10HP petrol engine and patent transmission to drive the wheels through a jack shaft and side rods (Plate 41). Although successful on trial, in practice they proved to be underpowered, have a transmission that needed skill to master, while the red hot glow of the exhaust pipe was dangerously visible to enemy snipers when working at night. Consequently, they were relegated to shunting at base depots or operating forestry tramways, duties at which they proved reasonably successful, fifteen more being ordered for similar work on the home front.

The second attempt at a 'tramway' loco was undertaken by the L.N.W.R. at Crewe works, who converted 132 Ford T cars into a convertible road/rail locomotive, a built-in turning plate being fitted so that only the forward gears of the car gearbox needed to be used when in rail form. This novel attempt produced a cheap, easily manufactured machine, but one only capable of hauling a very moderate load over the rough tramway tracks (Plate 24.)

Finally mention may be made of a few French-designed locos 'inherited' by the British Army when taking over systems previously worked by the French:– (1) the Pechot-Bourdon 0-4-4-0T, similar to the Fairlie but with only a single firebox without mid feather, designed in 1882 and built by Baldwin and North British as well as in France; and (2) Decauville 0-8-0T's, with outside cylinders and valve gear, and full length side tanks plus (in the Decauville examples) three additional water tanks between the frames, while the 70 similar locos built by Kerr Stuart in 1915–16 (their "Joffre" class) had only two additional tanks, and rode less well in consequence. No inventory of these locomotives (or captured German locos) used by the British has been attempted.

Disposals

Once hostilities ceased, huge quantities of light railway plant became redundant and needed disposal. This took around six years, most stock being sold off by private treaty, tender or auction in one of four ways:

(1) Locomotives (principally Hunslet 4-6-0T's and Motor Rails, plus a few Hudswell 0-6-0WT's) built too late for delivery to the front, together with those Baldwins and Alcos that had been sent to England for major repairs, were concentrated at a large dump at Purfleet Wharf, Essex and sold from there (see Appendix 3). By late 1919 no less than 255 steam and petrol locos were assembled here.

21. This picture (Q2813) of a working party of troops from the Kings (Liverpool) Regiment being conveyed in a train of Hudson 'V' skips, behind the front line near Arras on 28 June 1917, is an excellent portrait of the 'workhorse' of the WDLR, the 20HP Motor Rail 'Simplex' 4-wheel petrol locomotive.

Production of this design was due to the remarkable foresight of Mr T. Dixon-Abbott, Managing Director of the Motor Rail & Tramcar Co. Ltd. of Lewes, Sussex, who on seeing the vast stockpiles of light railway equipment in Germany before the War set about designing a cheap and simple petrol loco for British Army use. The essence of Dixon-Abbott's design was his patent gearbox which gave two speeds in either direction. Despite his pioneering efforts the war had run for nearly two years before the War Office was persuaded to take up his ideas, but once they did so both this and the larger 40HP type were produced in large numbers, up to 25 per week being built in 1918 once Motor Rail had moved to larger premises at Elstow Road, Bedford, and no longer sub-contracted final assembly. Essentially the locomotive consisted of a water-cooled two cylinder Dorman 2JO petrol engine transversely mounted on a channel steel, four wheeled underframe. Drive to the wheels was via chains through the patent gearbox. No cab was provided, the driver sitting sideways so he could see equally well in either direction. Motor Rail locomotives built today still use this basic design, a great tribute to the Company's founder.

This particular photograph was often used by Robert Hudson Ltd. to publicise their well known 'V' skips which they produced in huge numbers for the War Department, probably around 6,000 in all, most of which were for France. It seems probable the train in this photo was being used to construct the standard gauge line seen in the background. It is unlikely such a long train of skips would be needed for any other reason. A further point of interest is that the loco is numbered 364, a running number which cannot be reconciled with official records. (Imperial War Museum)

(2) Some locomotives, mostly petrol-electrics, plus 20 and 40HP Simplexes and a few Baldwins were apparently shipped back to Richborough Harbour early in 1919. The very poor results from the subsequent auctions did not encourage further shipments back.

(3) Many locomotives and almost all the rolling stock and track was sold direct from dumps established at bases in

France. The principal dump at Beaurainville (Plate 43) was later taken over by Robert Hudson Ltd. who continued the sales on their own account until about 1927.

(4) Some locomotives, probably those unsold at Purfleet and Richborough, seem to have migrated to various military bases in Southern England and were included in general disposal sales held there.

To sum up, most of the Hunslet 4-6-0T's and Simplexes found new homes, many being bought back by their builders for overhaul and resale. Many Simplexes were rebuilt as "Planet-Simplex" loco-

22. *An ex-Australian Army Barclay 0-6-0WT, its number obliterated, and disfigured with an ugly corrugated iron 'cab', at an unidentified location in France after the War.* *(R.T. Horne collection)*

motives by the Kent Construction and Engineering Co. of Ashford or their successors F.C. Hibberd Ltd. Known survival figures for the other types are rather less, particularly the Hudswell and Barclay well tanks, and it is difficult to determine how many were battle casualties, too worn out to find a buyer, or were sold but have not yet been traced. Resolving these problems remains a fascinating task.

Rolling Stock

The first wagons were crude affairs built by the troops themselves for the trench tramways, utilising locally acquired wheels and axleboxes. In March 1916 some standard Decauville bogie wagons were taken over along with the French Army system around Hersin and Saulty. From these, a standard bogie wagon (later known as class 'C') was evolved and built in Britain in large numbers, along with a 4-wheel open (class 'A') which had various identical components. With the big light railway expansion in Autumn 1916, Rendell Palmer & Tritton took the opportunity to design a completely new range of rolling stock, drawing on the experience in use accumulated so far. Mainstay of the range was the 'D' class bogie wagon, a highly versatile wooden bodied vehicle designed for heavy loads such as ammunition.

The same standard underframe was used for the 'E' and 'F' class drop side and bolster flat wagons (for bulky loads such as timber or fodder), the 'H' class water tank wagon, and a unique 6 wagon workshop train, consisting of a tool van, stores van with lockers and two swivel cranes, three machinery vans with a good range of small machine tools, and an office van with accommodation for those in charge and a petrol engine driven generating set, the whole train providing a comprehensive repair service away from the established depots. A few ambulance vans were built on slightly lengthened bogie underframes. There was also a range of 4-wheel wagons – principally the class 'B' 4-wheel open, an improved 'A' class, the class 'K' standard 'V' skip in 18 and 27 cu.ft. sizes and the lattice sided 'P' class ration wagon capable of being loco hauled or hand worked over trench tramways. Finally there were small quantities of various tip wagons, 'G' class tank wagons on 'A' underframes, and push trolleys of various types for the trench tramways.

Fourteen different British firms built WDLR rolling stock and, in constrast with loco design, they all built identical rolling stock from a standard range of drawings. Ironically as Robert Hudson's name is so associated with the bogie wagons, they only actually built a few 'H' class bogie water tank wagons, although they may well have been involved in producing the original design. Instead they mainly devoted their manufacturing resources to the production of 'V' skips and 20lb/yd pre-fabricated track, both for the WDLR and for contracting lines on the home front.

23. Once the 20HP Simplex had proved itself, the War Office asked Motor Rail to design and build a larger locomotive for use in the exposed front line areas. Their proposals for a 40HP locomotive were accepted immediately, production commencing in February 1917. Mechanically very similar to their 20HP forebears, they employed a four cylinder Dorman 4JO engine. The massive plate steel frame carried curved end shields of heavy gauge steel which gave protection to the internal mechanics and acted as ballast weights. The locomotives were built in three types: the 'open' locomotive having a simple awning mounted on four pillars, the 'protected' type also having shrapnel-proof side doors with adjustable visors over doors and end panels, and the 'armoured' type which was fully enclosed, resembling a contemporary tank in appearance (and adding 1 ton 2 cwt to the original 6 ton weight).

LR2223, Motor Rail 502 of 1917, an example of the 'protected' type, is seen in this picture being serviced at a forward area workshop (one complete Light Railway Operating Company, No. 28, was wholly dedicated to 'Tractor Repair', though 'Train Crew' and 'LR Operating' Companies would carry out their own routine servicing). MR502 was later one of a number of the class bought back by the makers from the French Disposals Board at Arras in 1924. Having been rebuilt and allocated the new works number 3664 it was sold later that year to W.G. Armstrong Whitworth & Co. Ltd. for a contract in New Zealand, probably the construction of the Taneatua to Paeroa railway along the Bay of Plenty in the North Island.

In service, driving an enclosed 40HP Simplex with the doors closed proved unbearably hot, and locos usually ran with the doors open. This seems to have been officially recognised by often painting the running number on the inside of the doors, as is seen here.   (Lens of Sutton)

24. An excellent study of one of the less successful WDLR designs the 'Crewe Tractor'. Built at the London and North Western Railway's Crewe works, allegedly at the inspiration of the LNWR Chief Mechanical Engineer's daughter, the aim was to produce a unit suitable for both road and rail use. The locomotive was based on the Ford Model T motor car, using a normal Ford T engine, gearbox and axles, with chain drive between front and rear axles and a built-in turning plate to allow the car to be lifted off the rails and swung round to face the opposite direction. 132 were built in 1916-17, numbered 1-132 on the bonnet sides (later renumbered 01-0132). They also carried, as in a road vehicle, a MT inventory number on the bonnet.

In addition to the 'cars', six Ford one-ton trucks were rebuilt for use in East Africa. These were not convertible road/rail locos but had a four-wheel carrying bogie at the front and a single spoked wheel at the rear driven off the normal Ford T rear axle. They were numbered 1 to 6 on the bonnet sides.

For the original 'cars' the LNWR engineers guaranteed a haulage capacity of 5 tons on a 1 in 20 gradient, and proved this on a test track at Crewe works. Unfortunately front-line permanent way was not up to Crewe standards, and in practice the 'tractors' proved to be useless in a load-hauling capacity. In this 13 March 1918 view (Q10716) at St Julien, 'banking assistance' is being provided by gunners as LR0287 starts to move a wagon load of 18-pounder ammunition. (Imperial War Museum)

25. The limited British advance on the Somme in 1916 left a German-held bulge between there and Arras, and an offensive was launched in April 1917 to straighten the line and to pave the way for an advance to Valenciennes. The initial attack was successful and by April 11th the front line had advanced about 4 miles. About 6 miles of the River Scarpe was in British hands, and R.E. troops of the Inland Water Transport Corps, using an improvised fleet of boats (some of which had been transported overland) maintained a regular service from the basin at Arras to the lock at Fampoux. In this picture (Q5828) taken on 22 April 1917 at Blangy, gunners of the Royal Field Artillery are loading shells onto pontoon boats – normally used for building temporary bridges – for transport up to the front line. The surrounding 'moonscape' shows the effect of the preliminary bombardment in which 2,879 guns (989 of them heavy) took part and in which the new British gas shells were used. The photographer has captured a passing train on a 60 cm. gauge line, recently laid (from the new appearance of the sleepers) along the riverbank. A 20 HP Simplex is hauling a train of Hudson 1 cubic yd. 'V' skips which were usually used to carry stone ballast.

Road maintenance was a constant task, and as early as December 1916 the British Army was called upon to provide metal for roads in the British sector, a demand then estimated at 3,370 tons daily. In peace time, large quantities of road metal were imported from Tournai and Quenast in Belgium, but as wartime demands increased, more quarries were opened up in France, many of these worked by British Army Pioneer and labour units. The 20 HP Motor Rails, weighing only 2½ tons, were the ideal locomotives for use on lightly laid temporary tracks such as this one. Three officers of the Cameron Highlanders 'hitch' a lift on the locomotive, and the R.E. driver is well equipped for a 'brew up.'   (Imperial War Museum)

26. Many of the troops employed on railway construction and operation were specially recruited from the ranks of Railway Company employees at home, and a 'comb out' of infantry and service units already in France produced a number of troops with an existing railway background. This considerably reduced the training requirement, albeit most of the recruits were from 'main line' Companies, and it must have required a major degree of mental adjustment to cope with the types of skills needed to operate a light railway. Nevertheless, having a nucleus of personnel familiar with such concepts as block signalling greatly facilitated the evolution of the (ultimately quite sophisticated) methods of despatching and train control in use on the light railways from 1917 onwards.

Not all railway servants, however, found their way into the R.O.D. or the L.R.O.C.'s: the troops in this picture (Q35478) are from the 17th (Service) Battalion, Northumberland Fusiliers (North Eastern Railway) Pioneers. The battalion was raised in Hull in September 1914, from employees of the N.E.R. They went to France with the 32nd Division but were employed as General Headquarters railway construction troops from October 1916 to June 1918. This undated photograph shows the pioneers engaged in more general maintenance work, typical of the uses to which the tactical railways were put. An unidentified Baldwin 4-6-0T proceeds towards the front hauling 'D' class wagons heavily loaded with trench construction material. The second wagon contains trusses used for revettment (vertical reinforcement of trench walls). Once the trusses were in place, duckboards (contents of the first wagon) would be laid to form a floor to the trench. The third wagon contains sandbags. This type of work, although unglamorous, was dangerous as it took place within range of enemy artillery. The troops are therefore well prepared, with steel helmets, and rifles to defend themselves if necessary.

(Imperial War Museum)

27. Whatever localised uses were made of 60cm gauge light railways, their primary purpose was to act as feeders to existing standard or metre gauge railways, which were only able to operate safely outside of enemy artillery range. This in turn meant that goods had to be trans-shipped from wagons of one gauge to those of another. Trans-shipment was the main reason for the demise of the narrow gauge railway in Britain, but in wartime, with plentiful 'free' supplies of conscripted labour the cost could be borne. By 1917 however it was becoming apparent that manpower resources in Britain and the Colonies were not inexhaustible, and the mounting casualty rates at the front meant that the demand for men was increasing while the supply was drying up. So, between January 1917 and January 1918 the British Adminstration at the Wei-Hai-Wei coaling station in the Shantung province of China recruited and transported a volunteer force of over 40,000 Chinese coolies. Known as the Chinese Labour Force, they worked under the control of British officers on line-of-communication work in France (including labouring work on railway construction projects).

In this picture (Q35467) Chinese labourers are carefully unloading 12″ calibre shells from a French standard gauge van into a 'D' class wagon, one of four 'standard' classes of bogie wagon, this type was designed to carry high-density loads of up to 10 tons. The capacity of these wagons was 12 rounds of 12″ ammunition, which in this case is being stowed flat, although smaller calibre shells could be stowed upright, greatly increasing the quantities that could be carried e.g. 210 rounds of 6″ or 450 rounds of 4.5″. To the left of the van doors stands a private soldier of the Royal Garrison Artillery, a unit originally employed to operate the coastal guns defending Britain, but later deployed in France with a variety of heavy equipment, including naval weapons mounted on railway bogies. (Imperial War Museum)

28. Experience of the Somme campaign showed that on a 12 mile front some 20,000 tons of stores had to be distributed daily beyond railheads. Some idea of the volume and diversity of the material needing to be transported may be gleaned from an inventory of stores exported from England to France during the single month of February 1917:

Cement 30,000 barrels
Wire entanglements 40,000 lengths
Corrugated steel sheets 1,000,000
Roofing felt 50,000 rolls
Screw posts 400,000
Wire netting 20,000 rolls

Wire weaving for trench boards 240,000 sq ft
Steel shelters 5,000
Water piping 175 miles
Water tanks 1,775
Expanded metal sheets 20,000
Rolled steel joists 26,000

Having reached the railhead, stores and ammunition would be transhipped into 60 cm. gauge trains, worked forward by 'main line' Hunslet, Baldwin and Alco steam locos to a marshalling yard such as this one at Elverdinghe, the rear area for the northern end of the Ypres salient. Trains would then be remarshalled into short rakes, each of which would be worked forward by a 20HP or 40HP Simplex under cover of darkness. Often these trains would travel coupled together to maximise line capacity, each Simplex and wagon(s) dropping off at the spur leading to its designated distribution point.

There is a wealth of detail in this 1917 view (Q35489). On the left hand line a train going away from the camera, hauled by a Baldwin, conveys mostly salvage, including used shell cases. Next to it is a train of 'D' class wagons behind a 20HP Simplex, containing ammunition, including some large calibre shells in the second wagon. On the next road is a train headed by another Baldwin, comprising five 'F' class wagons, loaded with cases of small arms ammunition, some of it stacked, rather dangerously, above the top level of the removeable stanchions. As in most WDLR wagons, the brakesman has no designated accommodation, having to perch precariously on the protruding end of one bogie. Behind are more 'F' class wagons laden with ammunition and (middle distance) a third Baldwin 4-6-0T. (Imperial War Museum)

29. The Canadians were great railway builders: some 12,000 men, including three battalions of Railway Construction Corps, a Railway Bridging Company and 13 battalions of railway operating troops were employed in France. As early as the winter of 1914-15 they were experimenting with crudely-built tramways in and around the front line, using 'scrounged' French Army material, or equipment constructed in Corps workshops. By the following year two Tramway Companies were operating as part of the Canadian 1st and 2nd Corps. 'Tramway' Companies also evolved in many British Army formations, and were principally used to build and operate lightly engineered lines close to the front line, distributing ammunition, rations, engineer stores, etc. There was obviously liaison where the 'tramway' lines ended and ROD/WDLR lines began, and a limited amount of through running of wagons where engineering standards permitted. The 'Tramway' units were later organised into 'Foreways' companies, of which the Canadian Company was easily the most efficient: in January 1918 they controlled 53 miles of track, on which they moved 1,058 tons of supplies daily – by contrast, 1 Company of the British Army, with 46½ miles of track, were handling only 380 tons (albeit with fewer personnel).

This Canadian Offical photo (C0813) shows .303 rifle ammunition being moved forward on an early light railway, following the attack by the 2nd Canadian Division on Courcelette on 15 September 1916. This is one of the earliest known photographs of a locomotive-worked railway on the Western Front, and the pristine condition of the 20HP Simplex suggests that it has only just been put into traffic. At this stage only 73 20HP Motor Rails had been ordered and a mere 33 actually delivered. As this loco is fitted with ballast weights it cannot be one of the first fourteen, so it must be in the series 214-232.

(Imperial War Museum)

30. The third Battle of Ypres began on 31 July 1917, in an area reclaimed from Marshland, the main thrust in the Allied attack being borne by Gough's Fifth Army. The British Artillery strength totalled 3091 guns (999 heavy) and in a bombardment lasting nine days fired off 4¼ million shells – 4¾ tons for every yard of ground. This was the first real test of the Light Railways' capacity to move large tonnages forward, and trains ran night and day to satisfy the guns' voracious demands. In this photo (Q5855) taken at Brielen on 3 August 1917, a train is arriving at an ammunition dump, set back slightly (for obvious safety reasons) from the guns, which are themselves sited about 8,000 metres from the German front line at this point. A mixed force of Royal Engineers and Royal Garrison Artillery troops are unloading the ammunition, mostly 9.2in. howitzer shells, for RGA ammunition columns to collect as needed. Note the empty shell! cases in the foreground: these were carefully salvaged and transported from France to Newport where a workshop inside the Great Western Railway Docks, covering 13 acres and employing 5,000 girls, reconditioned the cases for refilling with explosive.

The train consists of a mixture of 'D' and 'F' class wagons: the latter, having no sides (only stanchions around which ropes could be tied) were not designed to carry heavy and unstable loads such as this. However, in wartime, the capability of equipment becomes tested beyond normal design parameters, and so versatile were the 'F' class wagons that in 1918 some were strengthened to carry railborne artillery up to 8-inch calibre. The train is hauled by an Alco 2–6–2T and just in front (beyond the junction) is an 'open' 40HP Motor Rail. Photographs of the 40HP Simplex in this form in use in France are scarce, possibly because a number of the original 80 locomotives were later converted to 'protected' or 'armoured' types.

(Imperial War Museum)

31. *If Hell is as bad as what I have seen at Courcelette"*, wrote a Canadian officer in his diary, *"I would not wish my worst enemy to go there"*. Although 2nd Canadian Division, backed up by seven tanks, took Courcelette (an objective on the Albert – Baupaume road) in broad daylight on 15 September 1916, they were immediately counter-attacked and heavily shelled by German artillery, causing a large number of casualties. Some of these are being taken to a dressing station on a primitive tramway, typical of those employed by the British and Canadian Tramway Companies in the early stages of the War. Although the condition of the wounded seems desparate, many owed their lives to the speed at which even primitive railways such as this could move them to an ambulance station. The track is of the prefabricated type, using 9lb/yd rail, and follows the contours of the land. Few locomotives had been supplied at this time, and in any event they would not have been suited to such lightly laid and uneven track. Motive power on these tramways consisted of manpower, mules and (as here) heavy horses. The wagon being hauled is a home-built example, probably constructed in a Corps workshop, and would appear to employ Decauville wheels and roller bearing axle boxes on a wooden frame and body.

Trench tramways continued in use throughout the War, and even after the setting up of the WDLR continued to be widely used for movement of supplies and ammunition forwards from the start of the heavy artillery zone (about 5,000–6,000 yards from the front). Transhipment from the WDLR to the tramways took place at transfer points, where locomotive haulage ceased and responsibility for distribution was handed over to the Army Tramway Companies. Some of the lighter four-wheel wagons were allowed to run through from WDLR lines onto the tramways, but bogie wagons were never permitted to do so.

(Imperial War Museum)

32. Only six or so months later, the Light Railway Operating Companies were getting into their stride, and in this view (Q6226) taken on 29 April 1917 at Feuchy, east of Arras, casualties of the Third Army's Spring offensive are being loaded into a 'D' class wagon which has been quickly adapted to carry wounded on stretchers. Later, more sophisticated adaptations of both 'D' and 'E' class wagons were carried out, fitting them with internal racks which allowed three stretchers (and occupants) to be stacked one above another, thus enabling each wagon to carry six men. A framed tarpaulin roof, with side and end flaps, was fitted as weather protection.

As Feuchy had only been taken on 11th April, the railway is either a line laid quickly by the L.R.O.C. to service the advance, or may have been captured from the retreating Germans. Both sides made extensive use of captured track mileage, and in the closing stages of the War L.R.O.C.'s became adept at linking up with abandoned enemy 60 cm. systems in the least possible time. Peak of efficiency was probably achieved by 4th Army who, following an attack on 8th August 1918, transported their 'tractors' forward by road and put 15 miles of captured line into operation using German rolling stock!

The driver of the 20HP Simplex is evidently taking the opportunity to service his machine, the raised bonnet giving an excellent view of the locomotive's mechanics. The Dorman 2JO engine, with its two cylinders cast in one block and an integral cylinder head can be clearly seen, also the transversely mounted water pump driven off the timing gears and the Dixie magneto with its two ignition leads 180° apart. The Dorman JO series engine, first produced in October 1913, was very extensively used by the military, the two cylinder version powering the 20HP MR whilst the four cylinder 4JO version was not only used in the 40HP MR and almost all the petrol electric locos, but also in the Halley and Caledon lorries as well as a variety of stationary applications.

(Imperial War Museum)

33. The Canadians also operated 'ambulance trains' and this is an extemporised train consisting of a 'D' class wagon on which seriously wounded (including at least one German) are stacked on stretchers, plus an 'E' class wagon conveying walking wounded. The locomotive, a 20HP Simplex, is numbered 107. Several photos exist of these locomotives numbered in a 1xx series (which was originally allocated to the 'Hudson' 0–6–0WT's, see Appendix 1), but no official records mention this and it would appear to be a purely locally applied number. Note that the loco is a later WDLR example with cast iron sandboxes, as opposed to the pressed steel ones fitted to the 1916/17 20HP machines.

The picture (CO3333) is taken at Inchy-en-Artois, 10 km west of Cambrai on 27 September 1918, at the time of the Allied 'push' which finally broke the German armies' resistance and ended the War six weeks later. Casualties were heavy, and numerous prisoners were taken: two such, in the right foreground, await their fate.

After the War this very extensive 60 cm system in the Arras and Vis-en-Artois area was left intact and some 67 km was run as a public light railway by the Société Anonyme des Chemins de Fer a Voie de 60. By 1926 this had closed and the track at the Arras end lifted, much being relaid on the extensive Smiths Potato Crisps railways at Nocton, Lincolnshire. However the system around Vis-en-Artois was taken over by Société F Beghin for transporting sugar beet to the local refinery. This line was a veritable working museum of the WDLR with a huge number of ex-WDLR locos of all types except the Hunslet 4–6–0T and the 40HP Simplex, carrying beet in 'D' class bogie wagons over WDLR track. Tragically very few enthusiasts visited the line and almost everything was cut up, a notable exception being Alco 1265, which after further service at Pithiviers is now MOUNTAINEER on the Festiniog Railway. (Imperial War Museum)

34. In 1914, public opinion in the USA generally favoured the Allies, but there was a strong isolationist feeling and no desire to join in an Imperialist quarrel 3,000 miles distant. American industry, however, was quick to profit from the vastly increased demand for war material, which far outstripped what the factories of Europe could provide. Guns, ammunition and motor transport for the Allies began to flow across the Atlantic, and this was soon followed by railway equipment, in the form of Pechot-Bourdon type 0-4-4-OT's for the French, and Baldwin 4-6-OT's and Alco 2-6-2T's for the British. Little production capacity was left to supply the US's own Army, which was singularly unprepared when the USA declared war on Germany on 6 April 1917.

By 1918, railways were being operated by the First American L.R.O.C. and by numerous Engineers Battalions, for transport of troops and munitions and for logging operations (the latter used 3'0" as well as 60 cm. gauge equipment). However in the early days of American involvement, some US troops were assigned to British sectors to gain experience. In this September 1917 view at Boisleux-au-Mont (Q6075), men who were part of a regiment raised from the New York, New Haven and Hartford Railroad, learn the basic essentials of two-foot gauge railroading by sprucing up Hunslet 4-6-OT No. 303.

This particular locomotive is one of the few illustrated which definitely still survives today. It became one of seven of these locos which were bought back by Hunslet, converted from 60 cm. to 2 ft. gauge by pushing out the tyres and fitting new brake blocks, then resold to the Engineering Supply Co. of Australia. Most of these locos went to the Queensland sugar cane tramways, No. 303 (HE1215/1916) going to Bingera Mill, near Bundaberg in 1924, where it was named HUNSLET, working there until 1956. It was then purchased by Invicta sugar mill as their own Hunslet INVICTA (HE1226, originally WDLR 314) had a worn out boiler. INVICTA's cab and side tanks, complete with nameplate, were used to repair HE1215. The hybrid loco put in another eight years hard work, and after three years disuse was presented to the Rowes Bay Bush Children's Home, Townsville, in 1967 where it still rests.

(Imperial War Museum)

35. In the light of British Army experience,where the Alco 2–6–2T's had proved more serviceable than the Baldwin 4–6–0T's (especially when running bunker first), the US Army adopted the 2–6–2T wheel arrangement as standard. 195 2–6–2T's were built by Baldwins between September and December 1917. These, together with various petrol-engined machines, bore the brunt of the US Armies' narrow gauge railroad effort throughout and after the War (when the US forces assisted with reconstruction of devastated areas, and movement of displaced persons). However not all the Baldwins were delivered in time to see action: this photo (Q69533) shows nos. 5029 (BLW 45640) and 5043 (BLW 46503), built in September and October 1917 respectively, at the 19th Transportation Company Base Section No 1, St Nazaire, on 1st November 1918, still not fully assembled (note missing chimney on No. 5029). Pressure on shipping resources caused delays, it also appears that n.g. locomotives were piled in boxes on Baldwins' wharf in New York and were selected at random when a ship called – so locomotives built later in 1917 may have been shipped first.

In the closing months of the War, the US Army ordered another 100 2–6–2T's from Davenports and a further 130 from the Vulcan Iron Works, Wilkes-Barre. The Davenports were outshopped between October 1918 and June 1919, and 30 of the Vulcans in April and May 1919. (The balance of the order was cancelled, following a belated realisation that the War was over). Most of the Davenports were eventually scrapped, though some returned to the US where they were used for training purposes on a number of US Army camps until the 1940's.　　　　　　　　　　　　　　　　　　　　　　　　　　　　　　　　　　　　(Imperial War Museum)

36. As already mentioned, the Americans were able to benefit from their Allies' experience and order well proven equipment for their own light railways. For their standard petrol locomotive 126 machines were ordered from Baldwins to the same 7½ ton 45HP design as the 600 locomotives already built for the French Government artillery railways. Baldwins had been successfully building petrol locomotives as early as 1910 and by 1917 were able to offer a proven design with a four cylinder side valve petrol engine driving the locomotive via a gear box and jackshaft at the front of the locomotive and side rods to the wheels. When John Fowler and Co. Ltd. began building petrol locomotives a few years later they adopted similar ideas and may well have been influenced by Baldwin's designs. The 7½ ton locomotives were numbered in a series from 7001 on (Works no. 47126 – 47636, not continuous) and a batch of 72 locos to the same design were built by Whitcomb in 1920. Baldwins also built 63 smaller 5 ton locos which were numbered 8001 – 8063.

This USA Signal Corps photo (21712) shows three 7½ ton locos and a pair of Baldwin 2-6-2T's receiving routine maintenance in a rear area. Most US Army locos returned to the mother country after the War but a few Baldwin 2-6-2T's were used on French sugar beet lines and three more were bought by Penrhyn Slate Quarries in 1924. Intended to replace CHARLES, BLANCHE and LINDA on the main line, they just weren't up to the job and only lasted three years. However one of them (FELIN HEN, BLW 46828/1917) was later sold to the Fairymead Sugar Milling Co. of Bundaberg, Queensland, and after many years service, much of it running as an 0-6-2T, is currently undergoing restoration for museum use.

Although no US Army petrol locos came to Britain, two of the identical 7½ ton French locos did. One lasted at the Penlee stone quarries in the west of Cornwall until about April 1951, while Baldwin 49604 of 1918 is still in use in somewhat rebuilt form as the Festiniog Railway's MOELWYN.

(A Neale Collection)

37. The official caption to this photograph (E (Aus) 2787) reads "a light railway engine capsized while hauling a trainload of reinforcements to the front." The reality is less dramatic – Baldwin 4–6–0T No. 796 has derailed, a frequent occurrence as the light prefabricated points laid in the field were often not fitted with point levers, and movement of the blades could easily occur as a locomotive or wagon ran over them. Men of the Pioneer Battalion of the 3rd Australian Division are setting about rerailing the locomotive by jacking up the rear end, using sleepers as 'packing', to bring the rear wheels above rail level, at which stage the point blades can be reset and the loco lowered down onto the track. Men of the Light Railway Operating Companies became adept at this work, especially during 'front line' operations when trains ran during the night, and it was not unknown for locomotives to disappear into shell craters that had not existed on the outward journey! The action in this picture takes place at Harbonnieres, 8 km west of Villers-Bretonneux on the Somme, where the Australians fought the Germans to a standstill in the spring of 1918. Note 796's professionally built wooden cab, complete with rear 'spectacles' and hinged side windows.

The ability of the Baldwins to withstand this sort of regular punishment has contributed to their longevity – all the more astonishing for an 'asterity' design with a working life intended to be no more than a few years. Many of the industrial and agricultural lines on which they were later used had no better trackwork, and maintenance facilities were primitive to say the least, yet even today one or two survivors are still working on sugar cane tramways in India. (Imperial War Museum)

38. The caption to this picture (Q6849) taken near Sousstre on 16 July 1918, attributes the plight of Alco 2-6-2T No. 1247 to "sinking of the rails due to heavy rains." As in the previous picture, the caption is inaccurate. Both the Baldwins and Alcos were top-heavy, and inclined to roll alarmingly on uneven track (qualities that did not endear them to later owners such as the Welsh Highland). WDLR crews soon learned to restrict the speed of their progress to avoid derailments. Had the rails really sunk (and the crew not seen the danger in time), a disaster would have resulted, with consequences more serious than is apparent in this photo. What has in fact happened is rather more prosaic, and arises from a design weakness in both types of American locomotive. The side tanks, although capable of being filled separately, were joined underneath by a link pipe, intended to keep a common water level in each tank and so increase stability. However if a locomotive was left stationary for any length of time on track that was canted at an angle, water would drain from the 'higher' to the 'lower' tank, increasing the list and so accelerating the water flow. Eventually the increased weight of the 'downhill' tank would cause the loco to topple over! Damage would not usually be severe, if the locomotive decanted into soft mud, but re-railing could be a time consuming job.

Despite this little mishap, 1247 (Alco 57138 of 1917) was destined to survive another 40 years, being one of a very large number of ex WDLR steam and petrol locos employed at the extensive sugar beet railway of Societé F Beghin at Vis en Artois in the Pas de Calais, only being scrapped after the railway shut on the last day of 1957.   (Imperial War Museum)

39. Someone no doubt got a 'rocket' when this Ford Model T collided with a Dick Kerr petrol electric at Souchez on 7 April 1918, about 4 km. west of Vimy Ridge where the Canadian Corps had held the sector since their spectacular victory late in 1917. As enthusiastic light railway operators, the Canadians had gone further than anyone else and had actually built a proper 'office' coach on a bogie wagon underframe. A locally built timber body painted in ostentatious dazzle camouflage was fitted, with American-style roof, veranda for the brakesman, and fitted out inside as a mobile office with desks, filing cabinets and even curtains. Surprisingly, no other unit seems to have bothered with passenger vehicles at all, troops riding in open wagons or even skips, and officers travelling 'first class' on the locomotive. Even when King George V visited the Forestry Company troops in Hesdin Forest in August 1918 he had to be content with a crude bench seat fitted to an open four wheel flat wagon.

The locomotive in the picture (CO2562) is one of 200 petrol electric locos used by the WDLR. All sharing the same basic mechanical and electrical specification, the 100 built by Dick Kerr are readily distinguishable from their British Westinghouse counterparts by the louvred side bonnet panels and a different design of underframe.

The Ford Model T was widely used by the Allied forces. Apart from the 'Crewe Tractor' (see illustration 24) a number of T's were employed as staff cars, the 1914/1915 model shown here being a Canadian Corps HQ vehicle. From 1916 on large numbers of one ton Ford T lorries were also employed wherever local conditions made road transport practical. As a consequence even today France is still a happy hunting ground for Model T enthusiasts, with one ton lorries and the occasional car being regularly rescued for preservation. (Imperial War Museum)

40. Timber was required in enormous quantities during the four years of trench warfare. Large amounts were used to build 'corduroy' roads through the landscape shattered by war. Trench works required timber for revettment, construction of dugouts, tunnelling, wiring etc. Railways also absorbed large quantities in the form of sleepers. Up to the end of 1915, the French forestry department supplied all timber requirements from stock, but as demands increased the French allocated forest areas in which the British Department of Works made their own arrangements for felling. By the end of 1916, 13 officers (of the Works Directorate), five Royal Engineer Companies and 3½ labour battalions were employed on forestry work. Specially recruited Canadian foresters were also used, together with prisoners of war. In March 1917, control of forestry operations passed to a separate Directorate of Forestry, directly under the Quartermaster General. Monthly output of timber rose by the end of 1917 to 75,000 tons delivered to RE timber yards, and 25,000 tons to transportation store yards. Light railways were used extensively within the forests. Most were laid in light 9lb/yd rail and worked by men, horses or small petrol locos (see next illustration). In some areas however lines suitable for steam operation were laid down where timber had to be transported for any distance.

This 1918 picture (Q10244) shows a 60 cm. gauge line serving a sawmill in the Bretonne Forest. On the left, a Baldwin 4-6-0T has arrived with a load of rough timber. This would be unloaded by cranes or gantries and processed through the mill. In the centre, a steam crane operates on a crudely laid dual gauge line: the outside tracks (broad gauge) used by the crane, the inner rails used for carrying hand-pushed trucks for manoeuvering logs, and finished products, within the buildings. On the far right is a further complex of 60 cm gauge lines, probably serving another area of the forest.   (Imperial War Museum)

41. The Baguley petrol locos were designed to operate on the very light 9 lb/yd rails of the temporary trench tramways immediately behind the front lines. Two prototypes, Baguley 677 and 678 were ordered by the WDLR consulting engineers, Rendell, Palmer and Tritton on 3 January 1916 and delivered a month later. Despite satisfying initial trials at the maker's works, when a further 51 were put into front line service from June 1917, they proved totally unsuitable. Some were diverted to construction work on various UK military sites, the rest being mainly employed on forestry lines, shunting base workshops or other light duties in rear areas.

Although Baguley Cars Ltd. had taken over McEwan, Pratt & Co. Ltd. in 1913 the latter firm had earned such a good reputation that Baguley continued to build locomotives carrying the MEP name on their worksplate. 677 and its successors were solidly built four coupled locos with a Baguley 10HP twin cylinder petrol/paraffin engine driving the gears through Baguley two speed 'Patent' transmission and a jackshaft at the rear of the locomotive. The engine was a simple, robust water cooled side valve unit with a pair of cylinders with integral heads mounted on a cast iron crankcase, ignition being by Simms or Dixie magneto with a single Zenith carburettor. The large circular water tank used instead of a radiator gave the appearance of a steam loco, an illusion increased by fitting most of the WDLR locos with a brass capped chimney for the exhaust!

Few pictures exist of these locos in service but this one (Q10253) is one of several showing LR252 at work in the Basse Forêt d'Eu. The loco is presumed to be Baguley 684, a prototype sent originally to the Trench Warfare Dept at Audriq, near Calais, for evaluation, or Bg705, the second of the production WDLR locos (see Appendix 1). Rolling stock on this line consisted of Hudson platform wagons of very short wheelbase and unsprung roller bearing axleboxes. Such wagons were designed for hand or animal traction on very light track but could be used with light locomotives over short distances as seen here. Because of the overhanging load, a chain coupling is being used. (Imperial War Museum)

42. As already mentioned, both sides made extensive use of captured track mileage, since in rapid retreats there was usually no time to destroy permanent way. Priority was given to removing locomotives and rolling stock out of reach of the enemy: what could not be removed would be destroyed, locomotives usually wrecked by means of a grenade in the firebox. Sometimes however things did not go to plan and locomotives were captured in working order. In 1914 the initial German attack on Belgium succeeded in capturing many metre gauge locos, seriously hampering operations on the metre gauge lines still in Allied hands, and the Germans are known to have made use of captured French Pechot-Bourdons. Likewise, the Allies made use of captured German equipment, as much for its 'propaganda' value as for operational purposes (without a supply of spare parts, the life of a captured locomotive would be very short). American railroad troops made use of Deutz petrol locos and Feldbahn 0-8-0T's – even going so far as to number these in a US Army series with an X prefix.

British and Dominion troops also used the Deutz locos, and the Ministry of Munitions thriftily shipped some to Purfleet and tried to auction them after the War! (See Appendix 3). Some steam locos were also captured, and in this rare amateur photo, taken in the Ypres area in 1919, a German 0-4-0WT is being shipped off to an unknown destination. The loco is a Henschel 20HP 0-4-0WT, one of the maker's standard types. It is not one of the principal classes used by the German military railways, and may well be a contractor's locomotive used on an Army construction project behind the lines. Motive power is being provided by a Foden overtype steam wagon, owned by Woodhead Brothers of Silveroyd Hill, Armley, Leeds, who were steam haulage and steam threshing contractors. Bill Woodhead stands by the Foden's front wheel.

(Jack Walker Collection)

43. Light railway workshops were established initially at Berguette but when this area was threatened during the German breakthrough in 1918, the works were evacuated, stores and machinery sent to Zeneghem, and 60 cm. gauge locos awaiting repair sent to England. Early in May a site for new shops was chosen at Beaurainville, 7 miles east of Montreuil, and the plant and personnel reassembled. Repairs on locomotives and wagons recommenced in July 1918.

By September the Allies' rapid advance began to make narrow gauge railways redundant and depots such as Beaurainville were used to store surplus locos and stock. In this very interesting view (Q3668) of Beaurainville in winter 1918, a varied collection of locos has been assembled. On the left is a row of Alco 2-6-2T's while further to the right is a line of Hunslet 4-6-0T's and three rows of Baldwins. Of particular interest is the row immediately to the right of the Alcos. At the rear are five captured German 'Feldbahn' 0-8-0T's then come two 'Hudson' 0-6-0WT's, the nearest of which has had a steel back sheet with circular spectacles added to the standard half open cab. In front of the 'Hudsons' is a Barclay 0-6-0WT but the most interesting loco is right at the front. This is 218, one of two Hudson/Hudswell 0-4-0WT's delivered to the War office at Havre in 1916 (works nos. 1134 & 35). Of the maker's standard 'C' class with 6 in. by 9 in. cylinders and 1 ft. 8 in. diameter wheels, the point of interest is that they were built as 2 ft. 6 in. gauge. It can only be assumed that they were ordered when the War Office were still thinking of a few short, permanent lines built to the 'traditional' gauge of 2' 6''. At some time they were converted to 60 cm gauge but no details survive in the maker's records, so it may be assumed the work was carried out by the Army themselves.

The nearest Hunslet is No. 356, HE1268 of 1917, later sold to dealers George Cohen, Sons & Co. Ltd., Stanningley Plant Depot near Leeds, but whose ultimate fate is unknown.   (Imperial War Museum)

4-6-0 TYPE

SIDE TANK ENGINE

Gauge of Railway	1 ft. 11⅝ in. (60 cm.)
Size of Cylinders	9½ in. dia. × 12 in. stroke
Dia. of Coupled Wheels	2 ft. 0 in.
,, Bogie Wheels	1 ,, 6½ ,,
Rigid Wheelbase (Engine)	5 ,, 6 ,,
Total Wheelbase (Engine)	13 ,, 0 ,,
Height from Rail to Top of Chimney	8 ,, 11½ ,,
Extreme Width	6 ,, 3½ ,,
Heating Surface—Small Tubes ... 168 sq. ft.	
,, ,, Firebox ... 37 ,,	
Total ... 205 ,,	205 sq. ft.
Grate Area	3·95
Working Pressure	160 lbs. per sq. in.
Tank Capacity	375 gallons
Fuel Space (Coal)	15 cwts.
Weight Empty (Engine)	10 tons 18 cwts.
,, in Working Order (Engine)	14 ,, 1 ,,
Total Weight on Coupled Wheels	10 ,, 10 ,,
Maximum Axle Load	3 ,, 10 ,,
Tractive Effort at 75 per cent. of Boiler Pressure	5415 lbs.
Ratio Adhesive Weight ÷ Tractive Effort	4·34
Minimum Radius of Curve Engine will traverse with ease	100 ft.
Weight per Yard of Lightest Rail advisable	20 lbs.
Load Engine will haul on Level	286 tons
,, ,, ,, up Incline of 1 in 100	143 ,,
,, ,, ,, ,, ,, 1 in 50	80 ,,

*Code Word—***WAROFF**

C P 12 400/1/32

Order 37400

44. A loose leaf catalogue sheet for the 'War Office' class 4-6-0T, published by Hunslet after the War. Orders for nine of the type resulted: 4 for Nepal, 2 for Robert Hudson (Calcutta), 1 each for Australia, Chile and South Africa.

(Courtesy Hunslet Engine Co.)

WDLR Locomotive List

This Appendix lists all known locomotives delivered for use by the WDLR in France or other fronts. The lists are almost entirely based on surviving manufacturers' records and where information differs from that previously published it is believed the present version is correct. Apart from WDLR locos used behind the front lines the military authorities in Great Britain employed numerous new and secondhand locomotives of various gauges on such duties as forestry work and aerodrome, camp and dock construction contracts, but these have not been included. However, where such locomotives were included in an order for WDLR locos, reference to them will be found in the appropriate footnote.

Note: the title above each list indicates the working name used by L.R.O.C. personnel for that locomotive type, eg the Alco 2–6–2T's were known as 'Cookes'.

"HUDSON" 0-6-0WT

Specification: Hudswell Clarke Class 'G' 0–6–0WT standard design for Robert Hudson Ltd. 0–6–0 well tank; 6½'' x 12'' cylinders; 23 inch diameter wheels; 4ft 2in wheelbase; Walschaerts valve gear.

Works No.	Date ex Works	W.D. No.	Notes
1112	6/1916	101	(1) (5)
1113	5/1916	102	(1) (5)
1114	6/1916	103	(2) (5)
1115	6/1916	104	(2) (5)
1186	6/1916	105	(2) (5)
1187	6/1916	106	(2) (6)
1216–1220	7/1916	107–111	(2) (5)
1221	7/1916	112	(3) (5)
1226–1231	8–10/1916	113–118	(4) (5)
1232–1237	10–11/1916		(2) (5)
1256–1259	12/1916		(2) (5)
1260–1261	1/1917		(4) (5)
1265–1271	1–4/1917		(4) (5)
1272–1282	1917		(1) (5)
1291–1300	6–8/1917		(1) (5)
1318–1319	11/1919		(6)
1328	2/1919		(6)
1373–1374	2/1919		(6)
1375–1379	4–5/1919	3205–3209	(6)

NB HC 1301, 1302, 1310–1317 were identical locomotives ordered for military use in Great Britain and Ireland, mainly for aerodrome construction work.

Notes

(1) Despatched to the War Office at an unknown location but almost certainly used by the WDLR In France.

(2) Despatched to Dover Harbour for shipment to the WDLR in France.

(3) Intended to be despatched as Note (2) but commandeered for construction work at Richborough Harbour, Sandwich, Kent.

(4) Despatched to Salonika, Greece.

(5) WDLR 101 to 118 and all subsequent HC 0–6–0WT's for France were later renumbered, probably in a series from 401 onwards, but exact details are unknown.

(6) Ordered for use on the Italian front but due to the end of the War were stored at the W.D. dump at Railway Wharf, Purfleet, Essex, until sold from there. HC 1377 and 1378, were never delivered but sold direct to their subsequent owner, the Leighton Buzzard Light Railway Co., Ltd., direct from Hudswell's works, on 31 May 1919.

Hunslet "War Office" 4-6-0T

Specification: Hunslet 4-6-0T derived from the 'Hans Sauer' class 0-6-0T. 4-6-0 side tank; 9½'' x 12'' cylinders; 24 inch diameter driving wheels; 18½'' inch diameter bogie wheels; 5ft 6in coupled wheel base, 13ft 0in total wheel base; Walschaerts valve gear.

Works No.	Date ex Works	W.D. No.	Notes
1213-1222	10.8.1916-15.9.1916	301-310	(1)
1223-1257	29.9.1916-5.4.1917	311-345	(1)
1258-1287	24.3.1917-22.9.1917	346-375	(1) (2)
1295-1334	21.6.1918-30.1.1919	2323-2362	(3) (4)
1336-1375	2/1919-11/1919	3220-3259	(5) (6)

Notes

(1) Despatched to WDLR, France.

(2) Mechanically similar to HE 1213-1257 with minor exceptions, the principal one being the fitting of a water lifter and hose pipe.

(3) Intended for service in Italy and the Middle East but due to end of War only 14 (HE 1295-1308) delivered to Italy, and two (HE 1309-1310) to Palestine; the rest being stored at Purfleet Wharf, Essex.

(4) Mechanically similar to HE 1258-1287, except for minor modifications to drawgear.

(5) Due to end of War none of these locos saw WDLR service. HE 1356-1375 were all built to 2'6'', not 60cm gauge except HE 1356 which was modified during construction to 2'6½'' gauge and delivered direct to Jee's Hartshill Granite and Brick Co. Ltd., Nuneaton, Warwicks on 28 June 1919.

(6) HE 1354 and 1355 delivered to Royal Engineers Electric Light School, Stokes Bay, Gosport; HE 1354 resold to Hunslet Engine Co. in 1921, rebuilt with new boiler as HE 1454 for Nepal Govt. Forestry Railway, January 1923. HE 1355 transferred to Longmoor 1934, scrapped 1962.

BALDWIN 4-6-0T

Specification: Baldwin class 10-12-D 4-6-0T. 9'' x 12'' cylinders; 23½'' diameter coupled wheels; 16'' diameter bogie truck wheels; 5ft 8in coupled wheel base; outside Walschaerts valve gear.

Works No.	Date ex Works	W.D. No.	Notes
44335-44339	10/1916	501-505	(1) (2)
44351-44390	10/1916	506-545	(1) (2)
44489-44494	11/1916	701-706	(1) (2) (3)
44507-44556	12/1916	707-756	(1) (2) (3)
44635-44659	12/1916	757-781	(1) (2)
44681-44688	12/1916	782-789	(1) (2)
44695-44794	1/1917	790-889	(1) (2)
44891-44901	1/1917	890-900	(1) (2)
44938-45037	1/1917	901-1000	(1) (2)
45133-45236	2/1917	1001-1104	(1) (2) (4)
45374-45383	3/1917	1105-1114	(1) (2) (4)
45398-45433	4/1917	1115-1150	(1) (2) (4) (5)

Notes

(1) The first eleven locos of class 10-12-D were built for the Chemins de Fer Militaire de Maroc Occidentale (French military railways in Morocco) in 1916. Instead of the works number the expansion link of the motion was stamped with the consecutive number within the class (12 to 506 on the WDLR locos).

(2) The WDLR 10-12-D locos differed from the original Moroccan locos in having half instead of full cabs. From WDLR 855 onwards the centre driving wheels were flangeless and built in traversing jacks and steam operated water lifters were fitted.

(3) It was originally intended to number WDLR 701-715 as 546-560.

(4) During 1917 WDLR 1005-1150 were renumbered 546-700.

(5) Bwn 45414-45433 were apparently ordered as spare parts for other locomotives.

BARCLAY 0-6-0WT

Specification: Modified version of Andrew Barclay 'F' class 0-6-0WT standard design. 0-6-0 well tank with Belpaire firebox and outside valve gear; 6¾" x 10¾" cylinders; 20 inch diameter wheels; 4 ft. 4 in. wheelbase.

Works No.	Date ex Works	W.D. No.	Notes
1518-1542	2/1917-3/1917	601-625	(1)

Notes

(1) Some sources claim these locomotives were renumbered in an unknown series in late 1917 to avoid confusion with the Baldwin 4-6-0T's renumbered 546 to 700 but there is no definite evidence that this actually happened. The two locos (AB 1526 and AB 1535) which later saw service with Surrey County Council on the construction of the Guildford and Caterham By-Pass roads in the 1930's certainly retained their original cast iron number plates with the original WDLR nos. removed which suggests they were not renumbered. It is also worth noting that 25 Baldwin 4-6-0T from the batch WDLR 581-640 were sent from France to the Palestine front and if these were actually 601 to 625 (one was certainly 622) there would presumably be no need for renumbering.

ALCO "COOKE" 2-6-2T

Specification: 2-6-2 side tank by American Locomotive Corporation constructed at the Cooke Locomotive Works; 9" x 14" cylinders; 27 inch diameter driving wheels; 14 inch diameter truck wheels; 16 ft. 6 in. total wheel base; outside valve gear.

Works No.	Date ex Works	W.D. No.
57092-57191	24.2.1917-4.5.1917	1201-1300

"McEWAN PRATT" 0-4-0PM

Specification: Baguley 0-4-0PM powered by 10 HP 2 cylinder water cooled Baguley side valve engine with Baguley 2 speed patent transmission to jackshaft at rear of locomotive.

Works No.	Order Date	W.D. No.	Notes
677	3.1.1916	—	(1)
678	3.1.1916	—	(1)
682	28.3.1916	—	(2)
684	20.5.1917	—	(3)
704, 705	27.11.1916		(4) (5)
706, 707	27.11.1916	LP2264, LP2265	(4) (6)
708-713	14.2.1917	LR253-LR258	(4)
718	14.2.1917	LR259	(4)
721-730	14.2.1917	LR260-LR269	(4)
733-752	14.2.1917	LR270-LR289	(4)

Notes

(1) Prototype locomotives despatched 19.2.1916 (677) and 10.2.1916 (678) to War Office at unknown location for evaluation and testing.

(2) Despatched 12.5.1917 to War Office, Trench Warfare Dept, Porton, Wiltshire.

(3) Despatched 7.6.1917 to War Office, Trench Warfare Dept, Audricq, Calais.

(4) All these locomotives were despatched to the War Office, Calais for WDLR use between 12.6.17 (Bg 704) and 22.5.18 (Bg 752). They were part of an order for 49 locos (Bg 704 - 752), the remainder being employed on various military construction sites in the U.K.

(5) No WDLR nos. are known for these two locos but they were probably numbered LR251 and 252 (see Plate 41).

(6) LP is not a misprint, Baguley being ordered to number the locomotives as shown.

"CREWE TRACTORS"

Specification: Four wheeled convertible road/rail petrol tractor. Built by LNWR, Crewe Works using Ford Model T motor cars mounted on a steel underframe with 4ft 5in wheelbase. Ford T engine, gearbox and axles, with chain drive between front and rear axles and built-in turning plate.

Works No.	Date ex Works	W.D. No.	Notes
N/A	1916–17	1–132	(1) (2)

Notes

(1) Later renumbered 01–0132

(2) Also carried MT inventory number on bonnet

General note on the 'Simplex' locomotive lists

These lists have been taken from surviving Motor Rail records. It is often difficult to reconcile what MR recorded as actually being built with the Ministry of Munitions official orders. Before the 1914–18 War Motor Rail, which was founded in 1911 with a works at Lewes, Sussex, had only built tramcars and light rail cars of which very few records survive. Production of these locomotives was far beyond the capacity of their works and at first much of the work including final assembly was sub-contracted to the Bedford Engineering Co. Ltd., but in 1918 Motor Rail opened their own works at Elstow Road, Bedford and took over production entirely. It is believed that MR 842 was the first loco built by MR at Bedford. As noted in the lists, production of the last two batches of 20HP locos was curtailed due to the end of the War.

SIMPLEX 20HP TRACTORS

Specification: 4wPM by Motor Rail & Tramcar Co. Ltd. 20HP Dorman 2J0 two cylinder side valve petrol engine: Dixon-Abbott two-speed gearbox; chain drive to wheels; no cab.

Works No.	Order Date	W.D. No.	Notes
200–206	12.2.1916	200–206	(1) (2)
207–218	6.4.1916	207–218	(1) (2)
219–232	18.7.1916	219–232	(1) (2)
233–272	14.8.1916	233–272	(1) (2)
273–299	23.12.1916	273–299	(1) (3)
300–379	23.12.1916	LR1701–LR1780	(3)
842–1116	1.1.1918	LR2563–LR2837	(4) (5) (8)
1162–1255	23.1.1918	LR2883–LR2976	(5) (6) (8)
1642–1841	23.1.1918	LR2363–LR2562	(7) (8)

Notes

(1) The first 100 locos (MR200–299) carried running numbers that were identical with the works no. but without the LR prefix.

(2) Ex works date not recorded by builders.

(3) Ex works between 20.1.1917 and 17.3.1917.

(4) Ex works between 28.3.1918 and November 1918.

(5) These two batches of locos were part of larger orders which were not completed due to end of War. MR1117–1161 (LR2838–LR2882) and MR1256–1279 (LR2977–LR3000) being the locos not built.

(6) Ex works between July 1918 and late 1918.

(7) Ex works between early 1918 and 31.10.1918.

(8) Photographs show certain locomotives carrying numbers in the 1xx series painted on rather than the cast LR number plates normally fitted. This would apper to be a local renumbering and as far as is known all locomotives so numbered are among the three batches built in 1918.

SIMPLEX 40 HP TRACTORS

Specification: 4wPM by Motor Rail and Tramcar Co. Ltd. 40HP Dorman 4J0 four cylinder side valve petrol engine; Dixon – Abbott two–speed gearbox; chain drive to wheels; built as either 'open' 'protected' or 'armoured' versions.

Works No.	Order Date	W.D.L.R. No.	Notes
380–459	3.2.1917	LR2101–LR2180	(1) (4)
460–479	3.2.1917	LR2181–LR2200	(2)
480–595	25.10.1917	LR2201–LR2316	(3)
596–599	25.10.1917	LR2317–LR2320	(4) (5)
1280–1386	31.12.1917	LR3001–LR3107	(6)

Notes

(1) 'Open' locomotives, ex Works from 11.5.1917 on.

(2) 'Armoured' locomotives. Ex works after MR 380 – 459

(3) 'Protected' locomotives. Ex works 11.6.1917 onwards

(4) On 6.7.1917 the Ministry of Munitions ordered parts to convert an unrecorded number of 'open' locos to the 'armoured' type and on 4.8.1917 further parts to convert more 'open' locos to the 'protected' type. No details are available of how many or which locomotives were converted.

(5) 'Open' locomotives, ex works after MR480 – 595.

(6) 'Protected' locos. Ex works between July and December 1918. Due to end of War, only MR1280 – 1351 saw WDLR service, MR 1352 and 1353 being delivered to the WD tramway at Porton Camp, Wilts. Remaining 33 locos were stored at Purfleet Wharf, Essex, being advertised for sale in June 1919.

PETROL – ELECTRIC LOCOMOTIVES

Specification: Two types of four wheeled petrol electric locomotive utilising a 40 H.P. four cylinder Dorman 4JO petrol engine driving a 30 kilowatt generator, supplying current at 500 volts to two nose-suspended axle-hung traction motors; wheel diameter 2 ft. 8 in; wheelbase 5 ft. 6 in.

Works No.	Date ex Works	W.D. Nos.	Notes
—	Feb. 1917 on	1901 – 2000	(1) (2) (3)
Nasmyth Wilson 1144–1243	1917	2001–2100	(4) (5) (6)

Notes

(1) Built by Dick, Kerr & Co., Ltd, Preston with traction motors by Dick, Kerr and generator from Phoenix Dynamo Manufacturing Co. Ltd., Bradford.

(2) It was originally intended to number these locos 2001 to 2100.

(3) First three locos underwent trials on the North Wales Narrow Gauge Railway in February 1917, remaining 97 locos delivered direct to France.

(4) Ordered from British Westinghouse Ltd. who supplied the electrical equipment, generator and traction motors. It was intended that the mechanical parts should be built by Nasmyth Wilson. However, despite allocating works numbers to them as above, the latter subcontracted manufacture to the Leeds Forge Co. Ltd. Final erection was by British Westinghouse personnel in an empty workshop at West's Gas Appliances, Miles Platting, Manchester.

(5) It was originally intended to number these locos 1901 to 2000.

(6) Six locos had Tyler 45 HP engines instead of the Dorman 4JO.

SURVIVING EX-WDLR LOCOMOTIVES
PART 1 – UNITED KINGDOM

Note: All locomotives are Preserved unless otherwise indicated.

Type	Works No.	Date	Location*
Baldwin 4-6-0T	44656	1916	Chalk Pits Museum, Amberley, named LION
Baldwin 4-6-0T	44699	1917	Imperial War Museum, Duxford, named TIGER
Alco 2-6-2T	57156	1917	Festiniog Railway, named MOUNTAINEER (working)
Baguley 0-4-0PM	736	1918	Narrow Gauge Rly Centre of N. Wales, Gloddfa Ganol, Blaenau Festiniog (1)
MR 20HP 4wPM	246	1916	Ulster Folk Museum, Cultra, Co Down
MR 20HP 4wPM	?	1916	I.B. Jolly, Mold Clwyd (2)
MR 20HP 4wPM	872	1918	Chalk Pits Museum, Amberley (3)
MR 20HP 4wPM	997	1918	I.B. Jolly, Mold Clwyd
MR 20HP 4wPM	1111	1918	I.B. Jolly, Mold Clwyd
MR 20HP 4wPM	?	1918	I.B. Jolly, Mold Clwyd (4)
MR 20HP 4wPM	?	1918	Stornoway Waterworks, Isle of Lewis (4) (5)
MR 40HP 4wPM	460	1917	Midland Railway Centre, Butterley (6)
MR 40HP 4wPM	461	1917	Museum of Army Transport, Beverley
MR 40HP 4wPM	596	1917	Festiniog Railway, named MARY ANN (working) (7) (13)
MR 40HP 4wPM	1320	1918	Chalk Pits Museum, Amberley (7)
MR 40HP 4wPM	1363	1918	Unknown location, Bedfordshire (8)
MR 40HP 4wPM	1364	1918	Imperial War Museum, Duxford (6)
MR 40HP 4wPM	1369	1918	Armley Mills Industrial Museum, Leeds
MR 40HP 4wPM	1377	1918	National Railway Museum, York
MR 40HP 4wPM	1381	1918	Chalk Pits Museum, Amberley (9)
Dick Kerr 4wPE	—	1917	P. Rampton, Hambledon, Surrey (7)
'Planet' 20HP 4wDM	(Hibberd) 1887	1934	D. Preece, Callington, Cornwall (10)
'Planet' 20HP 4wDM	(Hibberd) 1896	1935	G.J.A. Evans, Launceston (10)
'Planet' 20HP 4wDM	(Hibberd) 1980	1936	Chalk Pits Museum, Amberley (10)
'Planet' 40HP 4wPM	(Hibberd) 1891	1934	Tarmac Roadstone, Wirksworth, Derbys. (5) (11)
'Planet' 40HP 4wPM	(Hibberd) 1612	1929	Chasewater Light Rly. Staffs (11)
'Planet' 40HP 4wPM	(Hibberd) 2914	1944	Chasewater Light Rly. Staffs (11)
Baldwin 0-4-0PM	49604	1918	Festiniog Railway, named MOELWYN (working) (12)

Notes

(1) At same locaiton are two other identical Baguley locos, nos. 646 and 760 of 1918, originally supplied to Government forestry lines in Britain.

(2) Precise identity unknown, believed to be MR264.

(3) Loco rebuilt by makers in 1926, now carries works no. 3720.

(4) Both these locos believed to be 1918 built WDLR locos but this cannot be confirmed.

(5) Derelict.

(6) Rebuilt to standard gauge.

(7) Rebuilt with diesel engine.

(8) Rebuilt by builders to 3'0'' gauge as MR3797 of 1926. Privately preserved.

(9) Restored as an 'open' loco, although built as 'protected' type.

(10) Rebuilds by F.C. Hibberd & Co. Ltd of ex-WDLR MR 20HP locos; all other surviving 'Planet-Simplex' 20HP locos are believed to be Hibberd-built locos, not rebuilds.

(11) Rebuilds by F.C. Hibberd & Co. Ltd of ex-WDLR MR 40HP MR locos to standard gauge. All now fitted with diesel engines.

(12) Built for French Army, not WDLR, but included for sake of completeness. Now rebuilt to 2-4-0DM.

(13) Although this loco now carries the worksplate from MR507 its true identity is as shown.

*Full addresses and other information on locations will be found in the handbook "INDUSTRIAL LOCOMOTIVES 1982" published by the Industrial Railway Society. Regular updates on changes in status of locomotives, movement between sites etc., are published in the Society's bi-monthly BULLETIN.

PART 2 - WORLDWIDE

Note: for status of locomotive(s) see appropriate entry or footnote

Type	Works No.	Date	Location
France			
Alco 2-6-2T	57148	1917	CF Touristique Froissy-Cappy-Dompierre (preserved)
Alco 2-6-2T	57131	1917	AMTP, Pithiviers (preserved) (1)
Greece			
Baldwin 4-6-0T	45010	1917	Volos (preserved)
Italy			
MR 40HP 4wPM	1294	1918	Italian State Rlys (FS),Electric Traction Depot, Bologna (2)
Portugal			
HC 0-6-0WT	1375	1918	CP (Portuguese State Railways), Porto Campanha (3)
Argentina			
Hunslet 4-6-0T	—	—	Santa Anna, Corrientes Province (BAGS No. 655) (4)
Hunslet 4-6-0T	—	—	Buenos Aires (BAGS No. 658) (4)
Brazil			
Hunslet 4-6-0T	1313	1918	Usina Leao Utinga, near Maceio, Alegoas State, named PAO AMARELLO (5)
Burma			
Hunslet 4-6-0T	1325	1918	Burma States Mines Railway (6)
Hunslet 4-6-0T	1326	1918	Burma States Mines Railway (6)
Hunslet 4-6-0T	1327	1918	Burma States Mines Railway (6)

India

Baldwin 4-6-0T	44696	1917 ⎫	Daurala Sugar Works, Daurala, Meerut (system closed)
Baldwin 4-6-0T	45190	1917 ⎭	
Baldwin 4-6-0T	44708	1917	Upper India Sugar Mills, Khatauli (system closed)
Baldwin 4-6-0T	45231	1917	BSSC, Motipur sugar mill (in use 1984)
Baldwin 4-6-0T	45380	1917	SKG Ltd., Hathua sugar mill (in use 1986) (7)
Hunslet 4-6-0T	—	— ⎫	Derelict at Coal of India Ltd., colliery
Baldwin 4-6-0T	—	— ⎭	near Chindwara, Nagpur (8)

Type	Works No.	Date	Location
Antigua			
MR 40HP 4wPM	466	1917	Antigua Sugar and Estates Development Board, Gunthorpes, Antigua (9)
St. Kitts			
MR 40 4wPM	435	1917)	St. Kitts (Basse Tierre) Sugar Factory Ltd. (10)
″ ″	452	1917)	
Australia			
Hunslet 4-6-0T	1215	1916	Rowan Bay Bush Children's Home, Townsville, Queensland (preserved)
″	1218	1916	C McLelland, Melbourne (preserved)
″	1229	1916	Australian N.G. Museum, Durundur Railway, Woodford, Queensland (preserved)
″	1239	1916	Langford Park, North Eton, Queensland (preserved)
″	1317	1918	Rotary Park, Prosperine, Queensland (preserved)
Baldwin 4-6-0T	45215	1917	Dreamworld, Coomera, Queensland (11)

General Note: This list of known surviving WDLR locomotives worldwide is almost certainly incomplete. Visits to many of the locations are few and far between, and published information fragmentary. The list has been based on published sources from 1975 onwards, and it is possible that some locomotives listed (especially in India) have been scrapped. Additional locomotives may exist, especially Motor Rail locos rebuilt by F.C. Hibberd or their predecessors as 'Planet' locomotives.

Notes

(1) Carries running number 3.22

(2) Rebuilt to standard gauge; departmental locomotive, now fitted with diesel engine. In use 1976.

(3) Now fully restored. Previously worked at Pejao colliery, Pedorido, near Porto. Mine and railway closed by 1972.

(4) Both locomotives built up from parts of a number of the 26 HE 4-6-0T's bought by Buenos Aires Great Southern Railway for use on their 60 cm. gauge agricultural lines. (Preserved).

(5) Loco rebuilt to metre gauge by Hunslet for this sugar mill in 1921, subsequently rebuilt to 0-6-2T. Rail system currently disused.

(6) Spares supplied by Hunslet for these locos in 1976, assumed to be still in existence.

(7) Rebuilt to 2' 6'' gauge.

(8) Noted here derelict in 1978, may have been scrapped since.

(9) Rebuilt by Motor Rail to 2' 6'' gauge for this sugar mill as MR 2177 of 1922; now fitted with diesel engine. Present status unknown.

(10) Rebuilt by Motor Rail to 2' 6'' gauge for this sugar mill as MR 3663 (ex MR 435) and MR 3666 (MR 452) of 1924 respectively. Present status unknown.

(11) Rebuilt to 'Wild West' outline circa 1975.

SURPLUS
RAILWAY MATERIAL SECTION
(D.B.2.c.).

*All applications should be addressed to the Controller,
Railway Material Section, Disposal Board, Ministry of Munitions,
Room 59, War Office, Embankment Annexe, London, S.W.1.*

THE FOLLOWING ARE FOR SALE BY PRIVATE
TREATY.

STEAM LOCOMOTIVES, 60 c.m. GAUGE.

14 Side Tank Engines.

Built by Hunslet Engine Co. Cylinders, 9½ in. x 12 in. stroke. Working pressure, 160 lbs. per sq. in. 4-6-0 type, having wheel base of 13 ft. 0 in. 5 ft. 6 in. coupled wheels. Weighing 14 tons in working order.

15 Side Tank Engines.

Built by Baldwin Loco. Works. Cylinders, 9 in. x 12 in. stroke. Working pressure, 178 lbs. per sq. in. 4-6-0 type, having wheel base of 12 ft. 2 in. 5 ft. 10 in. coupled wheels. Weighing 14.5 tons in working order.

1 Side Tank Engine.

Built by American Loco. Co. Cylinders, 9 in. x 14 in. stroke. Working pressure, 175 lbs. per sq. in. 2-6-2 type, having total wheel base of 16 ft. 6 in. 5 ft. 6 in. coupled wheels. Weighing 17.2 tons in working order.

The above are all lying at Purfleet.

2 ft. 0 in. and 60 c.m. Second-hand Steam Locomotives.

A number of the above gauge Engines, in good condition, of various types, by well-known makers, are now available.

STEAM LOCOMOTIVES, 2 ft. 6 in. GAUGE.

17 Side Tank Engines.

Built by Hunslet Engine Co., Leeds. Cylinders, 9½ in. x 12 in. stroke. Working pressure, 160 lbs. per sq. in. 4-6-0 type, having total wheel base of 13 ft. 0 in. 5 ft. 6 in. coupled wheels. Weighing 15 tons in working order. At present lying at the makers' works, Leeds.

PETROL TRACTORS, 60 c.m. GAUGE.

20 h.p. Petrol Tractors, "Simplex" Type. A Few New Tractors.

Built by "Motor Rail Co." 0-4-0 type, having wheel base of 3ft. 6½ in. Weighing 2.25 tons. In working order. Fitted with water-cooled Dorman engine. Two cylinders, 120 m/m x 140 m/m stroke. Normal full speed r.p.m. 1,000, having "Dixie" magneto ignition, forced lubrication. Inverted cone clutch drive. Two speeds, ahead and reverse. At present lying at Purfleet.

40 h.p. Petrol Tractors, "Simplex" Type, New.

Built by "Motor Rail Co." 0-4-0 type, having wheel base of 4 ft. 0 in. Weighing 6.3 tons. In working order. Fitted with water-cooled Dorman engine. Four cylinders, 120 m/m x 140 m/m stroke. Normal full speed r.p.m. 1.000, having "Dixie" magneto ignition, forced lubrication. Inverted cone clutch drive. Two speeds, ahead and reverse. Lying at Purfleet.

Quantity of Spares for do. (20 & 40 h.p. Dormer Engines.)

Lying at Purfleet. Dorman type.

180 h.p. Petrol Tractors, 4 ft. 8½ in. Gauge.

Built by "Manning, Wardle and Co." Fitted with Thorneycroft six cylinder Marine Type Reversible engine. 8½ in. x 12 in. stroke. Bosch Magneto ignition, water-cooled, having normal full speed of 550 r.p.m. Governor controlled and fitted with compressed air arrangements for starting and reversing. Power transmitted through three speed gear box, four coupled wheels, 6 ft. 0 in. wheel base. Total weight in running order approx. 27 tons. 2 lying at R. E. Stores, Purfleet (packed in cases), 4 lying at Richborough.

Captured German Tractors.

A number of slow-speed, single horizontal cylinder of the Gas Engine type. For low-tension oscillating magneto. Ranging from 15 to 40 h.p., driving through spur gears, giving two speeds in each direction.

60 c.m. GAUGE WAGONS.

Class A.

Four-wheeled open wagons, fixed sides and ends. 6 ft. o in. long, 2 ft. 6 in. deep inside. Tare, 16 cwt. 2 qrs. 20 lbs.; load, 3 tons 13 cwt. 1 qr. 8 lbs.; Total, 4 tons 10 cwt.

As above, with folding sides and ends. Tare, 18 cwt.; load, 3 tons 12 cwt.; Total, 4 tons 10 cwt.

Class D.

Bogie low-sided wagons, with falling doors. 17 ft. 6 in. long x 5 ft. o in. wide, 2 ft. o in. deep inside. Tare, 2 tons 5 cwt.; load, 9 tons 15 cwt.; total, 12 tons.

Class F.

Bogie well wagon, with detachable stanchions. 17 ft. 8½ in. long, 5 ft. o in. wide, stanchions 3 ft. o in. high. Tare, 2 tons 2 cwt.; load, 9 tons 18 cwt.; total, 12 tons.

Class K.

Double-sided tip wagons, one cubic yard capacity, suitable for running on rails 20 lbs. per yard. Capable of tipping either side. Bodies arranged for lifting off underframes, being tipped while slung, and for standing upright when placed on ground loaded or unloaded. Bodies of ¼ in. plate, with strong rims and reinforced corners. Fitted with spring draw gear and side brakes. Wheels 12 in. dia. Dustproof roller type bearings.

Class H.

Bogie tank wagons, without tanks, 17 ft. 8½ in. long, 4 ft. 11⅝ in. wide, 2 ft. 9 in. deep. Capacity, 1,500 galls.

Class P.

Four-wheel light ration wagons, 6 ft. 8 in. long x 4 ft. 10 in. wide, with falling sides, 1 ft. 6 in. deep, and loose end stanchions.
Spare wheels and axles with roller bearings for tip wagons.
Spare parts for all above-mentioned rolling stock.
The above wagons are specially high quality, narrow gauge rolling stock manufactured to War Office requirements, and lying at the R.E. Transportation Stores, Purfleet.

The Ministry of Munitions had been set up to control production of war materials and once hostilities ceased it acted as the main Government agency for the sale of the huge quantities of plant, materials and property surplus to Government requirements. The Government Property Disposals Board published at fortnightly intervals from 1919 until July 1923 a booklet entitled "SURPLUS", listing everything for sale from a complete Aircraft Factory down to Soldiers' boots (Old) Grade 5. Sales were by auction, tender, or by individual negotiation.

Most WDLR locomotives were disposed of direct from site in France or the other fronts, the main exceptions being those built too late to be delivered to the front, and the various locos (mostly Baldwin 4-6-0T's) which had been sent to W.G. Bagnall Ltd. at Stafford for major repairs to relieve the over-worked front line workshops, and which never returned to France. The majority of locos listed in 'SURPLUS' were therefore those used by the military in the UK. However pages 63-65 of the August 15 1919 issue of 'SURPLUS' were largely devoted to the sale of WDLR locos and rolling stock, and extracts appear above.

Of the 60 cm gauge locos lying at Purfleet, the 14 Hunslets will be some of HE 1311-1334 and 1336-1353 which never reached the front line (see Appendix 1). All 42 had been advertised in the issue of 2 June 1919 but were not necessarily at Purfleet. The 15 Baldwins and the Alco were probably among the 21 Baldwins and several Alcos rebuilt by Bagnall and will include at least four of the Baldwins that subsequently worked in Britain*. The 2'0'' gauge locos were those used on construction work, depot railways and forestry lines in the UK. The 2'6'' gauge locos are 17 of the last 19 Hunslet 4-6-0T's (HE 1357-1375), built as 2'6'' gauge rather than 60 cm as by then the War was over, and the W.D. thought this would make them more saleable. Presumably they were right as two had been sold in the previous fortnight and all subsequently found new owners in India, Singapore and South America. Like the Hunslets, the Motor Rails listed were brand new locos that never saw active service, the 40HP machines being 'protected' types from the batch MR1280-1386 while the 20HP locos could have been from any of the last three lots built (see Appendix 1).

Also advertised are six of the ill-fated standard gauge Manning Wardle four coupled petrol locomotives. Twenty were built but the poor performance of the first ten meant that the second batch were confined to UK duties. The six listed will be from this batch (MW1945-1954 of 1918, MoM numbers 1691 to 1700) and appear to include four employed at Richborough Harbour and two intended for overseas service but never sent.

The attempt to sell captured German Deutz petrol locos found little response, even though some similar machines had been built for British customers before the War. One is rumoured to have been bought by Hudswell Clarke, as a source of knowledge for their projected range of petrol locos, and another may have gone to a South Humberside brickworks, but with so many new and secondhand Simplexes available at bargain prices the MoM had to look elsewhere for customers.

*Bwn 44383 and 44522 that later went to the Snailbeach District Railway; Bwn 45142 sold to the British Standard Cement Co. Ltd. at Rainham, Kent; and the Glyn Valley Tramway's Bwn 45221, although the latter may not have gone through Bagnall's works.

Bibliography

Internal Combustion Locomotives	Baldwin Locomotive Works Record No. 95 1919
Baldwin's Contribution to the War Effort	Baldwin Locomotive Works Record 1919
Light Railway Material (Catalogue 44795)	R. Hudson Leeds circa 1926
Official History of the Great War – Transportation on the Western Front	Col. A.M. Henniker HMSO 1937
History of the Corps of Royal Engineers – Vol. 5	Inst. of Royal Engineers 1952
Light Railways of the First World War	W.J.K. Davies; David & Charles 1967
The Leighton Buzzard Light Railway	S.A. Lelux Oakwood Press 1969
Railways and War Before 1918	D. Bishop and W.J.K. Davies Blandford Press 1972
The British Internal Combustion Locomotive 1884–1940	Brian Webb; David & Charles 1973
Baguley Locomotives 1914–1931	Rodney Weaver Industrial Railway Soc. 1975
Famous Regiments – the Royal Engineers	Derek Boyd; Leo Cooper 1975
Two-Foot Rails to the Front	C.S. Small Railroad Monographs 1982
The Patent Narrow Gauge Locomotives of J.B. Fell	E.A. Wade Narrow Gauge Rly. Soc. 1986

Periodicals

The Locomotive Magazine	October 15 1915
	January 15 1917
	May 15 1917
	September 14 1918
	October 15 1918
	June 15 1920
	September 14 1946
Industrial Railway Record	No. 65 April 1976
The Narrow Gauge	No. 76 Summer 1977
	No. 80 Summer 1978
	No. 82 Winter 1979
Model Railways	April 1976
	July 1976

ABOUT OURSELVES

Plateway Press was founded in 1986 by two committed enthusiasts, Andrew Neale and Keith Taylorson, to publish good quality material on neglected aspects of the railway and transport scene, with an emphasis on narrow gauge, minor and industrial railways. The operation is run from premises in Croydon astride the route of the erstwhile Surrey Iron Railway – an early railway or 'plateway' from which our name was derived.

Our aim is to publish books, drawings, postcards, etc., which contain accurate, well researched and original material. "NARROW GAUGE AT WAR" is our second book, and others are in preparation. We would be pleased to hear from any author or researcher who may have suitable material for publication, and we can offer help and advice on presentation.

If you would like to be included on our mailing list for advance news of future projects, please send a self-addressed stamped envelope to the address below.

ALSO AVAILABLE . . .

WAR DEPARTMENT LIGHT RAILWAYS POSTCARDS

An ideal complement to "NARROW GAUGE AT WAR", these Limited Edition black and white postcards depict steam and petrol locos in use on the W.D.L.R. circa 1918. Using views never before published on postcards, they are printed to a high standard, with captions on reverse, and each set is accompanied by a descriptive leaflet. Locomotives featured are:- 'Hudson' 0-6-0WT; Barclay 0-6-0WT; Hunslet 4-6-0T: Baldwin 4-6-0T; Alco 2-6-2T; 'Armoured' Simplex 4wP; captured German Army Deutz 4wP.

Price:- £2.00 per set of eight cards.

NARROW GAUGE AND MINIATURE RAILWAYS FROM OLD PICTURE POSTCARDS

This book explores the world of Narrow Gauge and Miniature railways through the medium of old picture postcards. Over 100 pictures – taken from old picture postcards published from about 1900 up to the present day – illustrate a diverse selection of narrow gauge, fifteen-inch and miniature railways. Coverage includes famous lines such as the Festiniog, Isle of Man and Ravenglass & Eskdale, and lesser known systems such as the Sand Hutton, Groudle Glen and Ashover Railways (whose Baldwin 4-6-0T is featured). A chapter is devoted to military railways, including the 1'6'' gauge system at Woolwich Arsenal. Most of the postcards are reproduced 'actual size' and accompanied by lengthy, authoritative captions. Appendices provide details of the railways featured, and of the postcards, their publishers, and their value to collectors.

"A well produced and original little book" (SLS JOURNAL)

"The quality of reproduction is generally excellent" (RAILWAY MAGAZINE)

"Andrew Neale has produced a highly entertaining volume . . a real treat at a bargain price"

(NARROW GAUGE NEWS)

Card covers, 9½'' x 6½'', 60 pages, 2 colour and 103 b/w illustrations

ISBN 0 9511108 0 2   Price: £4.95

All items Post Free from:-
    Plateway Press, 13 Church Road, Croydon, Surrey, CR0 1SG